HOW TO CONTROL YOUR FINANCIAL DESTINY

JENNIFER LANCASTER

Published by Power of Words. Clontarf, Qld, Australia.
www.jenniferlancaster.com.au

Disclaimer: This book is written as an educational guide only and does not constitute financial advice. While every effort has been taken to ensure all material is correct and up-to-date, the publisher/author takes no responsibility for errors or omissions. Each individual's situation is different, and all readers should seek professional consultation before undertaking any investment-related strategies suggested herein. The author accepts no legal responsibility for the performance of any investment tools suggested herein. The author does not receive any commissions or benefits from any organisations mentioned.

Lancaster, Jennifer (Jennifer Lee), 1971- .
How to Control your Financial Destiny. 3rd edition.
1st edition called 'Sack Your Financial Planner' (2008)

ISBN 978-0-9945105-7-0 (paperback)

About the Author

Jennifer Lancaster spent fifteen years of her adult life working, travelling, studying, and shopping. Then she met the man of her dreams, had a baby, got married, stayed home, and had to stop spending... well, mostly! Not to let an opportunity slip by, she wrote of her tricks to save money in a little book, *'How to Kick Bad Spending Habits'*.

In 2006, the Lancaster family moved to Redcliffe, Queensland, to find an affordable home near the beach. While getting organised and saving, house prices moved up 20%. What a great time to buy (not!). After purchasing a mortgage, the GFC hit, taking the regular business income away, so the couple worked hard in new service businesses.

Money kept in their offset account home loan came in handy in the down-times, as did their built-in 'granny flat'.

Now, with two different businesses and royalties, the stability of having multiple sources of income has helped even out the inevitable bumps of life.

"Like many, becoming financially independent is our goal".
– Jennifer Lancaster.

Other titles by Jennifer Lancaster:

Creative Ways with Money

Create your New Life of Abundance

Power Marketing: An Aussie Guide to Business Growth

How to Start a Freelance Business (ebook)

The Niche Marketing & Book Guide

Contents

Introduction: The Right Mindset

Most of us would like to be financially independent on retirement, yet few retirees achieve it. In fact, only about 6% of Australians are financially independent or wealthy. On retirement, the majority of seniors go from being independent to being financially dependent in some way.

While some retirees are proudly self-funded, most cannot sustain their former standard of living, surviving on a meagre portion of their previous salary. Because it is difficult to achieve ongoing passive income, we come to accept such a poor standard. Here are some startling statistics:

* 1 in 3 senior Australians live under the poverty line[1].
* Average superannuation balances at the time of retirement (age 60 to 64) in 2015-16 were $270,710 for men and $157,050 for women (ASFA reports).

Whereas wealth can be measured by net worth (assets minus debts), financial independence means not only money, but also freedom and control. We would probably all like to have the ability to control our financial destiny!

So how rich are we? Preliminary 2020 data says Australian households have median household wealth of $632,200[2], with

---

1 Oct 2020, The Australian, Global Age Watch index.

2 Dec 2020 ABS, Household Financial Resources. ABS.gov.

most of this being from property assets… as the value of owner-occupier homes continues to rise.

> *Households that owned their home outright (2.7 million households) had an average net worth of $1,237,000.*[3]

So, what is financial independence?

I believe it is enough income to meet all of your needs – and some of your wants – without any assistance, be it from employer, government or family. It could be less than what you needed when you were working or it could even be more, if you have grand plans.

It's obvious that many people want to improve their wealth, or at least their outlook. Millions have read the bestsellers, "Rich Dad, Poor Dad", "Think and Grow Rich", "Automatic Millionaire", etc… So why don't more people invest for the future?

It's probably because they're too busy spending it, thinking that they just cannot affect their own wealth. It seems shocking to me that many individuals who earn well over $85,000 per year admit that they *can't save anything*. In fact, many are loaded with personal debt in their peak earning years. It's almost like they have given up on allocating portions of their income to their various goals.

This may be reflective of a particular attitude to money – one author calls it a 'money personality'.

---

[3] ABS, Households Net Wealth and Distribution, 2019

"If you understand the why, the how (of money) is much, much easier. You need to consider your core motivations, psychology and general approach to money – and how that differs to your partner."

– Greg Smith, author of Unlock Secrets of your Money Personality

Even though you may either be a spender personality or have a spender telling you to "lighten up, have fun and don't worry about saving", if your goal is to invest for the future, it's important to make the necessary adjustment. Sorting out your wants from your needs is imperative to keep on financial track.

If, after finetuning your monthly budget, you still feel that your regular pay is simply too low to put aside some, then why not offer your own talents and knowledge in your after-hours by writing, designing, or training/coaching others. It's important to save for times when you cannot work.

"Immediate gratification cost you your wealth, but long-term, methodical, strategic vision builds wealth" – John Demartini

Excuses, Excuses!

What other common excuses are used to avoid starting to invest? "I don't have time for all that research", "it's risky", "I'm too in debt", "my wife/hubby is in charge of that department", "I'm going to win Lotto", "I'll die before retirement", etc. We're going to refer to Lotto winners in a moment, but let's cover some of those other excuses now.

Investing is risky

Compared with buying furniture or cars on credit (a sure-fire way to lose money), investing in growth assets is much safer: at least there is a good chance that the money will still be there next year!

The risks are more to do with the investor's ignorance or greed (or combination of all three), than with the investment. Some people make money no matter which way the market swings!

I'm too in debt to invest

Much of the middle class in Australia use credit for consumer goods, whereas the rich use loans to build assets that will continue to grow, in order to support their lifestyle. Some families spend **110%** of their total household income!

Accepting consumer debt as the norm, a lot of people just go get another loan or credit card transfer when they don't have enough money for what they want. It takes a paradigm shift to start to see debt as leverage to build wealth, rather than as 'lifestyle' money.

If you are motivated to get on track, then once you commit to the discipline of paying off as much as possible, you'll find it's easy to continue the habit of automatically putting aside that amount each month.

I'll talk more about debt later, since the pressure of housing and personal debt keeps many families from getting started.

It is not how much you earn, but what you do with it that counts.

I'll die before I retire

In all probability, you will most likely survive to face retirement. Life expectancy improves with age, so for example, a man born in 1960 who has reached 45, can expect to live to 72.4. But a female born in 2010 has a life expectancy at birth of age 84.3! [4]

Even before normal retirement age, an unforeseen event may make you realise that you've neglected financial planning for too long… you and your family must struggle just to sustain your usual standard of living.

Health should be a number one reason for financial planning, including emergency funds. Suffering early-onset heart disease and cancer is a reality for many people, and it pays to plan ahead so you don't have to rely on always working hard.

The Right Mindset

Belief in your investing abilities comes from small successes… experimental forays, not giant leaps. Expand your comfort zone slowly. Reading or hearing about similar people to us helps us believe we can do it too. We don't learn as well if we think the teacher is far beyond us; they must be grounded. That said, ensure

[4] Life Expectancy tables, Australian Bureau of Statistics, 2013a

you are paying the teacher for education and not being led into any particular investment.

Start to bring people around you that are positive and enhance your self-worth. They will recognise your efforts to change.

---

*A **poverty mindset** seeks problems. A **wealth mindset** seeks solutions.*

An example is, a poor mind worries about the damage tenants could do so avoids investing, and a rich mind finds ways to minimise the risk, like landlord's insurance, building insurance, and ensuring thorough checking of tenants' history.

Some people believe that there are *secrets to wealth* that can only be learned in seminars or workshops led by 'gurus', or by buying a 'trading system'. Sure, you can learn some honed tactics from them that may or may not work for you, but overarching 'secrets' – probably not. Secondly, even if you spend thousands on wealth creation courses, you may still fail because your mind was not prepared for success.

Learning is best done in stages, with some practical experience, and this usually takes time. Think of when you started learning to drive. It was not like you were a Formula One champion after the first lesson; you had to master some unfamiliar skills, learn the road rules, and get experience... just like investing!

You'll want to get your financial tuition from the most independent sources you can find. Local libraries offer some book choices, and others that delve into various investing areas can be sought online. The Australian Stock Exchange also offers free online courses (http://www.asx.com.au).

When learning, keep in mind the Chinese proverb:

"He who asks is a fool for five minutes, he who doesn't ask remains a fool forever".

The Dangers of Being Led

Gaining wealth is mostly a slow process for those patient and dedicated enough to delay gratification. Seeking riches quickly and without planning will normally ensure reversion to poverty just as quickly. A prime example is Lotto winners. A lot of large sum winners revert to their prior lifestyle five years later.

One of our biggest human weaknesses is the desire for easy riches. ACCC reports that $176 million was lost to scammers in 2020, a 23% increase over 2019, based on investor victim reports to Scamwatch. It's bigger than that, though; $328 million was lost in all investment scams in Australia. Unexpected prize scams amount to $1.7 million, while email payment redirection fraud cost businesses $128 million. The biggest cohort for losses was those 65+.

It doesn't have to be a scam either; there are many dangers in investing without education and self-determination. Retirees lose their life savings in failed mortgage debenture schemes, novices are lured into buying off the plan in a boom without their own research… These are examples of how women and men give their power away, believing that a financial spruiker knows better than they do about where to invest their money.

Hidden traps, credit pitfalls, and unfair practices are costing every hard worker many thousands of dollars as well. Ordinary Australians wishing to do all the good things like save for retirement, enjoy some passive income, and manage well financially, are being driven to the brink of financial disaster by simply being uninformed.

There are many reasons behind personal financial disaster. Over-borrowing without a contingency plan plays the second largest role in financial hardship. (Unemployment or loss of income plays the largest role). In 2020–21, there were 10,621 total new personal insolvencies (a fall of 49%); consisting of 6,792 bankruptcies, 3,731 debt agreements.[(5)]

It never pays to invest in something you don't understand. In 2007-09, tens of thousands of fixed interest investors did not understand the risk they carried. Mortgage fund/unsecured debentures investors in Provident Capital, City Pacific, Allco Finance, EquityTrust, IM Investment International, were all promised high returns that disappeared in their collapses. Many lost 30 to 90 per cent of their capital... and with gearing, some lost it all. (Borrowing can compound losses).

A fund reliant on borrowings and in-flows (as in mezzanine finance) is way too complex for the average or even the above-

---

5 Australian Financial Security Authority, AFSA.gov.au, Annual Statistics 2020-21

average person to calculate the risks adequately. In assessing a new investment, always question why this fund offers higher rates of interest than the banks. What underlying risk is it carrying?

The Two Sides of Housing Debt

Over the past 25 years, household debt has increased nearly twice as fast as the value of household assets (ABS). Recently, the RBA found that the household debt-to-disposable income ratio was at 181% in March 2021. That means we Australian adults carry 1.8 times the debt as we have the ready income to service it and keep living. Ouch! [6]

Our house prices are above the US, at 5-6 times annual income or more, making it hard to afford a first home. You can see by the chart overleaf that as housing prices rise, our overall debt ratio also rises.

Although the debt level is high, apparently it doesn't mean anything regarding economic fundamentals:

> *"There does not appear to be a level at which bad things start to happen" – Ian MacFarlane, Governor, Reserve Bank of Australia*

[6] BusinessInsider.com.au, Household debt levels record lending, 2021.

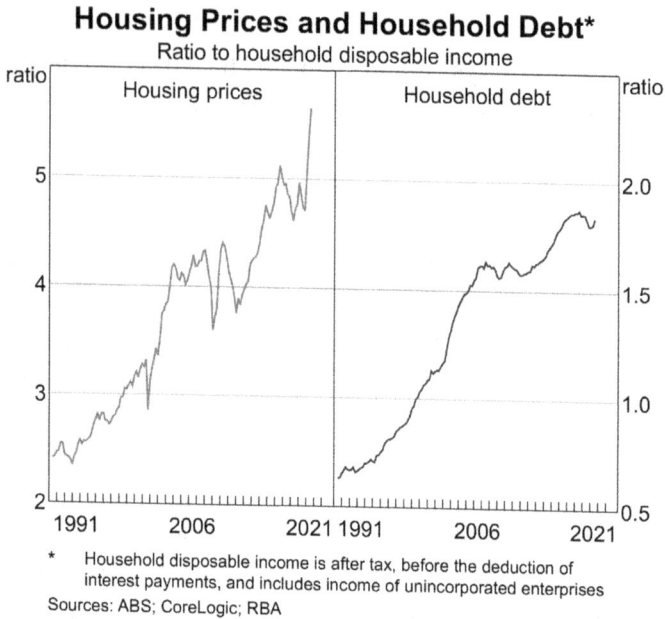

For those with good income, this high leverage worked well for many years. Those who invested in a holiday house, residential or commercial property, or a farm, had their increase in overall real wealth grow faster than their debt over 2003 to 2004.

But then, as properties in cities got ever more expensive, household debt nearly doubled between 2003-04 and 2015-16. Growth in household debt (including personal credit) became larger than the growth in income and assets over that time. ABS calls this 'over-indebted households', and this unlucky number climbed to 29 per cent of all households with debt (2015-16) and half of all mortgage holders.[7]

[7] ABS, 6523.0 - Household Income and Wealth, Australia, 2015-16

The increase in the Australian household Debt-to-Household Income ratio is higher than in most other countries, and in 2018 it sat at 190 per cent.[8]

Those with another property besides their own residence benefited from a steady increase in equity, contributing 27 percent of the real increase in their overall wealth between 2003-04 and 2011-12[9]. It was a good time to hold property, regardless of any particular location knowledge.

It would be folly to think that these capital gains would be as easy to achieve as during a boom time. As they always say in disclaimers: "Past performance is no guarantee of future performance." Yet you can't sit back in fear either because nobody achieved his or her desired financial destiny without taking a risk of any kind.

If you're dedicated to work, you seek a basic personal finance education, create a clear goal-based strategy that considers the risks, then you will soon be on your way to financial freedom.

Learning Points:

* While some just give up without trying, if you want to retire financially independent then you must make a strategic plan!

* Success with investing depends a lot on the investor's mindset. Wealthy people keep risks down rather than letting fears stop them, so you must do this too.

---

[8] RBA Research Discussion paper, 'How risky is household debt?' 2020.

[9] ABS Trends in Household Debt, 2013

* Get your financial education from independent sources, not spruikers.

* Investing in anything without knowledge of what it is can prove risky; but you can get personal finance and investing knowledge for free at your library or online at the Stock Exchange.

* Over the past 20 years, Aussies have wielded the weapon of debt (for real estate) to build personal wealth, but now the younger set are carrying too much debt.

* The patient will grow their net wealth and passive income; those seeking instant riches will lose much of their savings in one way or another.

Growing an Income for Life

Do you really want to rely on the Government and compulsory Superannuation to give you a meagre income… with only a tiny pension at retirement? Women and men now in middle-age have to await the pension age of 67 in Australia.

If you procrastinate financial planning, you may well have to work on well into your seventies, ask for handouts, or live frugally. ASFA says a single needs $45,962 per year and a couple needs $64,771 per year for a comfortable retirement.

And so, planning for a passive or semi-passive income is probably the most important step in the process of setting up for retirement.

A passive income comes in regardless of your everyday work, and that's why it's a preferred form of income. The trouble is, most people don't think about the need for this, let alone plan to buy assets that will later spit off passive income.

Women especially tend to prioritise others in their family, some taking a break mid-career to have a child, others unsure about personal finance decisions, and so the majority do not have a plan for their financial future.

Many women are left in a perilous financial position through the sad events of death, illness or divorce, often at a time in their life when they cannot save up again. Some must flee the home, without any money, and some had an addicted partner who spent all the assets away. These are the stories behind the statistics.

How can you remedy this situation? Firstly, by assessing your attitudes to risk and reward and creating a plan that is aligned with your values. Secondly, by finding your innermost reasons to create lasting financial security.

Lastly, by learning about investing through reading widely and 'having a go' yourself. It's probably best if your first investment is a smaller one that is easily sold, such as ETFs or shares.

However, some retirees are determined and goal oriented. Despite her husband's initial grumbles, one New Zealand lady in her mid-60s planned for a comfortable retirement by targeting renting out cottages and built-in flats on their paid-off farm. The husband retired from farming at 70. Rental income now totals about $840+ a week, without sowing a crop. There is no debt; one 'bach' (cottage) cost only $12,000 second-hand, including house moving, another was a flat initially built for the eldest child, and another was a garage and second bathroom that was converted to a flat.

This landlady understood about the demand for housing in their local town and ensured they offered clean, affordable accommodation. The husband no longer grumbles as he shares the loot in exchange for keeping it all running. It's a great way of keeping their much-loved farm while still affording the huge upkeep bills as they get older.

Of course, these folk are my parents! Can you see how these low-cost assets with no debt, means greater passive income? It's kind of opposite to how we are taught by professionals, with high debt being their only answer. Something like 70 percent debt/30 percent equity may be needed to get your assets built up, but on retirement the equity level needs to be a lot more, ideally all paid off.

Merely accumulating a large lump sum in our Super/Pension fund to use as a source of income in retirement is perhaps the wrong focus. For some, with not as many years left to build a huge sum, it's very hard to make up for lost time. It's also unwise to think everything will stay the same and let you live on $500,000 for 23 years. After all, you/your spouse might need nursing care. Sometimes dividends and interest have a low period, so capital is eaten at a higher rate.

Diversity is a must for retirement, since a stockmarket downturn can spell disaster for some who are relying on investments to live. Similarly, security lovers often find very low fixed interest rates difficult to live on. So it makes sense to actively control your assets in the safest and best yielding environment at the time.

How do I become Financially Independent?

One option for the young is a savings and interest reinvestment plan, continued through many years. The average university graduate will earn $2-3 million dollars in his or her lifetime. Compounding their savings for 40 years will usually equate to an adequate nest egg.

For those of us who are middle-aged, there are other strategies.

Some wealthy investors actually use the increasing equity in their properties for spending money (by drawing down loan funds). This generally takes portfolios of $1.5 million+. Other active investors have bought enough assets to maintain their lifestyle through cash flow. Here are three possible ways to become financially independent:

a) ***Capital gain***. Pay down your mortgage in the main, and with the equity, invest wisely in strong capital growth investments (shares or property), negative gearing at first, then paying out debt later by reinvesting income or gains. Then live off the increasing income and equity; or

b) ***Cash flow***. Invest wisely in positive cash-flow properties or businesses that pay you a small return, adding more over time with the slowly growing equity, and on retirement sell a few to pay down debt and gain a better income stream; or

c) ***Leverage your business***. Set up franchising in your own business, if it proves a success and replicable. After a period, get in a manager and this will give a residual income. Alternatively, grow your business and sell for a profit (capital gain).

Ultimately there are only two modes of investing on which to focus depending on your aims: *cash flow* or *capital gain*. If you want to acquire assets for a positive cash-flow (money in your pocket after expenses and deductions) from day one, your investment choices will differ from those who seek to gain capital from markets trending upwards and do not mind having to input cash from their primary income.

Investments don't discriminate, people do. Anyone can do it.

Saving is Not Investing

Many people think they have done well in squirreling some cash into a fixed interest term deposit and leave it at that. Saving involves making disciplined choices in spending and this is not easy. While I endorse a saving ethic, saving is not the same as investing. *Money* author David Potts says, "***Investing is buying assets that will increase in value***".

The main reason to graduate from merely saving to investing is to grow wealth through assets. Unfortunately, with savings in bank accounts, term deposits or bonds, your cash barely grows, and can even go backwards, with inflation erosion and tax. (See *What is the Real Rate of Return*).

What is the Time Value of Money?

Net present value (NPV) is a simple way to work out what the value of money will be in future, versus what it would be worth if received today, also accounting for inflation and interest payments. This can help answer these types of curly questions:

> Should I withdraw my nest egg today, or leave it to compound and only draw down its income?

> Should I put my excess $500 per month into my Superannuation, or pay down my mortgage or other debt?

The Time Value of Money, or TVM, is a principle that explains how time affects the value of money. The concept is simple: *"A dollar today is always worth MORE than a dollar tomorrow."* (Investopedia.com)

This is because interest can be earned from the day you receive the money (e.g. receive $1 million inheritance now + 5% fixed interest = $1,050,000 in your account after one year). For spenders, there is a huge caveat to this idea, as money withdrawn is quite likely to be spent!

Another practical application of this principle concerns foreign exchange. Say you are considering transferring the money from overseas to pay down your loan. Consider the amount of interest payable that you would SAVE over the time in question if you received the money sooner (and not just the currency exchange rate).

Say you want to save a $1 million for retirement with the help of compound interest. You put $5,000 into a high-interest online account (or Superannuation if you're 40+). You automatically pay $300 per week into the account over 25 years, and on average, the account earns 6 per cent interest. Who needs wine, gambling, latest gadgets and designer clothes anyway? Wallah... you'll have $1 million dollars in 25 years. Ah, but what will that be worth then?

To think of it in today's terms, an inflation calculator has output this:

Amount: $1,000,000

Annual inflation rate: 3%

Number of years: 25

Reduced amount: $477,605.57

Required amount: $2,093,777.93

Oops, you thought you'd be quite wealthy. While $477,000 today is an okay nest egg for one, it would not represent what you were aiming for.

Other things to consider are **risk of capital**, annual **fees** and **market downturns**, particularly because when your nest egg gets up in value you may well be tempted towards the sharemarket rather than fixed interest.

Remember, money is just a way of keeping score!

What is an Asset?

Some authors believe that your home is not your greatest asset; it is a liability. Yet it is not black and white; the equity in your home can be considered an asset when it comes to lending against its increasing value, while any mortgage remains a liability.

Robert Kiyosaki's rich dad put it this way, "*if you stop working, an asset puts money in your pocket, while a liability takes money out of your pocket". (Rich Dad, Poor Dad).*

Assets can include profitable businesses, properties (land, residential, commercial), managed funds, derivatives, hedge funds, private equity, shares, gold bullion (no income), and sometimes art and antiques (although these cannot be borrowed against).

Your car is not generally classed an asset to a lender, but it could be an asset to you, as you could sell it. Ensure you use the current market value in calculations and not the price you paid.

Learning Points:

* Determine your own risk comfort levels, based on the past. Do they need updating to meet your current goals?

* What are your reasons to create financial security?

* Cash flow or capital gain – determine which you want to start focussing on.

* Retirement income needs means reducing your debt and increasing equity, so plan to pay principal and interest on any investment loans pre-retirement.

* The value of money reduces over time, so we need to be smart with investing it to keep in front.

* Saving is not enough; investing in assets that increase in value is required for financial independence.

Planning Ahead and Knowing Yourself

Investing well requires a financial education, especially if your goal is financial freedom. Other steps are goal setting, making an action plan, monitoring and fine-tuning, and sometimes changing course.

Imagine you are about to embark on a long sailing journey. You've heard of this idyllic island, sunny and warm. You want to be prepared. You read up on boating (education). You hire or buy the right boat that will deal with the high seas (the wealth vehicle), you chart your course on paper (plans/goals), and you examine the risks and prepare for them. Before you even set sail, you visualise yourself landing on the tropical island. When you see a storm brewing you don't sail into it 'hoping for the best', you reset your course, perhaps taking longer but knowing it is a safer path. You then arrive in one piece, ready to enjoy those sunny days.

But first, you need to know where you are now. Get out your pen (or use an online net worth calculator) to create a **Net Worth Statement**. List your wealth as Assets less Liabilities, and Income less Expenses. This gives lenders and financial people a view of your financial situation. A current valuation of your property is needed for correct asset calculation, or for a rough guide, use www.HomePriceGuide.com.au.

Financial statements, like an Assets & Liabilities and Income & Expenses statement, help you as well. It helps you to focus on growing ASSETS, adding passive INCOME, and reducing variable EXPENSES. This is how the rich think, and this is how they got rich.

Thorough financial planning is key to controlling your financial life, yet many of us put off making any written plan for ourselves, or we think we need a $10,000 'wealth plan' from an expert. I hope you come to realise that *you* (and your spouse) are the best ones for the job of your family's financial planning.

You will find a form as the basis of a simple financial plan in the Appendix. It really only takes one or two hours every month to keep track of how you're generally travelling toward your goals (net worth). Every year, shop around for better banking and insurance products or possibly super funds, and check the commissions or ongoing fees.

Many sports pros spend all they earn. Three years after retirement, about three-quarters are struggling. So the answer is not in having more money coming through your hands. But if you build up a high net worth and assets, you have more financial security as you can usually sell an asset in times of crisis. Salaries, in contrast, can be cut without warning or health can fail.

Risk Profile: Which are You?

Are you scared to invest in anything other than fixed interest, capital guaranteed funds or bonds? You are a *Conservative* investor.

Do you like a balance of assets that give a better likelihood of some growth without much loss? You are a *Balanced* investor.

Do you seek out capital growth investments to control yourself, and can tolerate some capital loss to achieve more gains? You are an *Active* investor.

Do you speculate to seek strong profits, risking your capital, and seek advanced styles of investing? You are an *Aggressive* investor.

These are just loose categories, and there is nothing to say that with a little education and practise, you couldn't move into a different style of investing that's more likely to meet your goals. For example, a couple who saved conservatively for many years realise that their retirement will be dismal just on fixed interest income, so armed with more knowledge, they carefully invest in high-demand, high yielding property at a 80:20 loan to value ratio. Over time, this builds a passive income they can live on.

Some people expect great rewards without taking *any* risks, and that is not how the financial world works. Risk and reward are normally closely linked. Nevertheless, there are strategies to reduce risk that you may not be aware of yet. Even *having* an investing strategy equates to less risk, and puts you in front of the punters.

FAQs about Strategy…

Q. *Should I be looking at investing in growth shares or funds in my senior years, to make up for poor performance?*

A. No, at 60 years of age or so, there is not enough time in your earning years to ride out another slump in the sharemarket. At most, put 50/50 into defensive assets (like fixed interest) and growth assets (like property or blue chip shares that pay franked dividends). And remember to check your Super Fund allocation; often 'balanced' options are 70 percent invested in slightly riskier, growth assets, like shares.

Learning Points:

* Financial Statements (Assets & Liabilities, Income & Expenses) helps you to focus on growing ASSETS, adding INCOME, and reducing EXPENSES. So get onto an online budget planner (Budgetpulse.com) and get all the calculations done for you.

* What kind of investor are you… Balanced, Conservative, Active or Aggressive? Will that style at your time of life meet your future goals?

* Risk and reward are linked, so having a personal investing strategy with risks in mind is going to put you in front.

* Know your investing time horizon – how long have you got left to ride out the ups and downs of the market before retirement? Or can you build up a retirement passive income to counteract market ups and downs?

Financial Professionals: their Wealth... or Yours?

Financial advisers, stockbrokers, mortgage brokers, bank staff, and property development salespeople do not normally know you well enough to advise exactly what is right for you. They can only give you investing alternatives, loan guidance and specific product information; they cannot decide for you the right course of action.

Sometimes of course you will need to use financial services and take the advice of accountants, but if you already have a plan, it makes it so much easier to keep on track and fulfil your goals.

Financial Planners

A financial adviser/planner has traditionally been a salesperson on commission for financial products, e.g. managed funds. Today, 80 percent of financial advisers still make money from upfront commissions, mainly from insurance products. Many flog these continuously, since earning commissions on insurance is allowable. With all the one-eyed advice by those in finance today, you are likely better off seeing yourself as CEO of your own finances… providing you further your financial education and keep up-to-date.

Financial planners were always required to assess your attitude to risk and be up to speed with legal/tax changes, but with the Future of Financial Advice reforms in 2013, advisers were also required to:

* Offer advice in your best interests only
* No longer be paid a commission by product (fund) providers
* Send an annual fee statement to clients, and request feedback about clients wanting continued advice, and
* Not make money out of trailing commissions.

So, the reforms have encouraged financial advice to be paid for upfront, surely a good thing. Our current federal government is busy repealing some of these points, and now advisers can avoid full disclosure of fees.

As you might expect, financial planners dropped off like flies as these reforms moved into place. Unfortunately, with high-cost alternatives, it makes it harder to access good financial advice for those in the low to middle income brackets. Hence the need for this book and many like it.

SuperGuide (.com.au) has a list of just 43 independent financial advisers in Australia, although this is not an exhaustive list.

What do Financial Planners charge?

Generally, you can pay about $200 per hour for a Financial Planner and $100 p.h. for a Paraplanner (less qualified person). These days an initial plan fee usually covers identifying your needs, developing a strategy, and implementing the recommendations. (It's still not as much as some wealth coaches charge – up to the $10,000 level). For a high-income earner, it is likely worth paying out for the plan fee, *if* all of your considerations are taken into account, as high flyers don't have the time to research every angle.

Free, simple financial advice can be found within mutuals / banks, managed funds you own, at your life insurance provider, or with your superannuation fund. Some industry super funds provide free webinars on retirement planning.

What do I look for in a Financial Planner?

Check for an Australian Financial Services (AFS) License issued by ASIC, and as added security to comply with ethics, look for FPA (Financial Planning Association) members. Never get financial advice from overseas brokers of any kind.

Property Education Groups & Companies

A common question on investing forums is this:

These Property Cash Flow people say they are mentors and will help me retire early... are they really Property Mentors?

The huge commissions available in new property can often bias investment advice. In the property investing market, be wary of 'property investment consultants' who want you to inspect and buy one of their recommended houses very quickly. They might proffer education, but how are they making their money? Is there a transparent fee (good) or are the costs hidden in overpriced houses (bad)? Do they let you get a fair valuation arranged or use your own accountant if you want a second opinion?

There are also many property education groups. The people at any property group are in business to make a profit. As a client, you'll have to pay for that service in one way or another, but you may get swept up in the enthusiasm of the group or its leaders and make a hasty decision. The leaders will push you to do it their way, yet only YOU are responsible for creating your own destiny. Indeed, you are the one servicing the loan.

Of course, it's easy to get caught up in great promises of wonderful financial rewards and a fast track to early retirement. For most, it doesn't happen that easily or quickly. By all accounts, the path to wealth requires specialist knowledge and a lot of persistence. While progress may seem slow, working to your own objectives for wealth, work and family is bound to be a better route for you.

A property group (that's run for profit) may still be able to help with your education, as long as you keep doing your own research. Another alternative is to pay for training by an experienced property mentor in a particular investing approach. Make sure they have some good case studies, which let you know all the details of their clients' success. You can also invest through your own family/friends in a properly set up property co-op, although you need an agreed exit plan for this.

> *"If you buy a property for investment, the best advice is to seek advice from someone who is not getting a financial benefit from your purchase" — Neil Jenman (Real Estate Mistakes)*

What about Other Professionals' Investing Advice?

Even Real Estate Agents with no investing experience will deem to advise you what is a good investment. Remember, they are working for the seller and for their own interests. A Buyers Agent, on the other hand, works for you to buy the best value property to suit your needs. They must also have a real estate licence.

When 'financial people' of any kind call me, I am on red alert, because I learnt early on that some offers really are too good to be true. In 1999 I was a naive investor who bought shares in an off-market US company (now defunct) through a notorious Thailand broker called The Madison Group. They never let you sell. These brokers were referred to me by a friend, which is a common occurrence in these hard-sell scams. Yet losing your money does not take you off the scammers' calling list. I was later approached by a 'New York-based' broker to buy my worthless stock. *Huh?* I thought. Nothing came of it, but at least I didn't lose more money.

Along with a healthy dose of scepticism, your mind must be business focussed to do well at investing. Perhaps imagine you are a top manager of a fund yourself. If a new opportunity comes to light, put your 'business hat' on and research the organisation thoroughly, going over the market sector, earnings forecasts, debt, dividends, company stability, and analysts' recommendations. Then decide the percentage of your portfolio they can occupy. As a guide, astute investors usually risk no more than 10% of their total capital on any one company.

Of course, some people do not have enough money for a diverse share portfolio of six to ten companies. One alternative for those with smaller amounts of capital is investing in **ETFs** (Exchange Traded Funds), which are normally diversified but core in one area (e.g. High Yield, Emerging).

Or, diversifying across your own Superannuation fund is another option, with its low tax environ. You can choose classes like 'infrastructure' or 'property', offering diversity and better returns than cash. There are some ETFs that only require $1,000 to start. Find out more in Chapter 12: *Managed Investments*.

> *"Investing is a business — a business that most advisors know little about" — The Meridian Business Group*

Financial Coaching... an unbiased alternative

Wealth or financial coaching is another way of professionals helping hard-working Aussies get ahead. They can help with managing personal debt, laying out a financial plan for wealth and passive income, and providing financial education to fill any gaps in knowledge. You usually pay up-front or monthly. Ensure the level is appropriate to your overall resources for investing.

Investment group mentoring is a similar personalised way to learn, but with a group of others meeting regularly. Ensure this is real education and not a sales fest for properties or something else.

If mentoring is based on a property investing strategy, then ensure there is a proven system and ongoing help that is worth the fees, and you have a choice of property that suits your budget.

Learning Points:

* Always think about the underlying motives of any financial person giving you advice.

* You are the best person to plan your family finances and set goals.

* Try to get independent or at least uncommissioned advice – you might have to pay for this advice.

* Be business minded in your investment due diligence.

The man who says it can't be done should not interrupt the person doing it. – *Chinese proverb*

Income, Expenses and The Gap

Firstly, Mind Your Business

You would like to have more income before you save and invest, right? *If* you keep your spending the same, increasing your income can make a power of difference. Of course that's very hard on hourly wages. You need to think like an entrepreneur.

Take a look at your attitudes to risk and security. Increasing wealth involves taking on a little more calculated risk than usual.

This does *not* mean trusting what salespeople are telling you and letting greed influence decisions. Write down what you are afraid of and research each point in turn, uncovering historical facts and figures.

Examine whether you want to gain **more cash flow**, or whether you can wait and would rather build net wealth through **capital gain.**

Expand your horizons with a spare-time **hobby that can make money**, e.g. selling your handmade crafts, helping others to learn English, writing an ebook in your field of knowledge and selling it online, selling furniture you found, for a profit. Return the costs to yourself, declare any profit on your tax return, and put after-tax profits into your 'future fund'.

And for established business operators:

> **Use proven systems in order to leverage your income** streams, e.g. franchising your business, planning the acquisition of good cash flow assets, or partnership deals, etc.
>
> **Reach more people** that can sell your products through affiliates (online) or referrals (offline). Offer incentives like discounts or commissions. Work on expanding your networks through clubs, networking breakfasts and industry associations. Mention your enterprise, and how it helps people, to everyone.
>
> To improve business growth, **learn about good sales and marketing methods**. You could go to local State Development & Trade workshops (search for "Small Business Solutions"), as these are inexpensive, methodical and offer some mentoring.
>
> There are also free seminars about web and digital marketing in each regional area, put on by local experts. (More marketing advice in '*Power Marketing*').

A Salary Rise isn't Going to Help

You probably think that the simple answer to your money worries is to ask for a raise, or perhaps wait for that inheritance. But think about what generally happens when people get a raise or bonus. Off they go and buy something they've been wanting, such as new clothes or a new car. They'll go out to dinner more often or go on more expensive holidays. So when income goes up, household spending goes up, without even thinking consciously about it.

You're smarter than that, so when you expect more money to come in, plan for an increase in automated savings, e.g. take it from 5 percent to 10 percent but *keep your monthly budget the same!* Then you can use it later for investment in income-producing assets.

Next, Mind Your Expenses

Advertising attempts to weave a spell that keeps the middle class living perpetually in bad debt. Through personal experience I found that 'saving' money by buying brand goods on sale does not put you ahead. You can really save your money by:

* Budgeting and planning instead of impulsive buying
* Taking a business approach to household expenses and trim costs where you can. Compare contracts to pay-as-you-go for energy, gas, mobile phone, home phone, and internet access.
* Using discount chemists, buying petrol off-peak, taking holidays off-peak, using your present health fund entertainment discounts, buying insurance online, etc.
* Scouting around for good second hand bargains.
* Buying in bulk the basics your household always uses.
* Not using a credit card if you can't pay it off monthly.
* Not blowing *all* your savings on your holidays!

Keeping a 'Spending Diary' (recording everything you spend for at least a week) and creating a detailed monthly budget planner makes you realise just how much is thrown away on incidentals (e.g. coffee, fake nails, muffins, beer, trashy mags) that could instead set you up for the future.

Are you amazed at how fast your cash withdrawals go? Can't believe how many items are on your account statement? Perhaps see ANZ's online program at MoneyMinded.com (the Money Leaks part) and then put in how you are going to replace your daily indulgences more cheaply. Consider replacing pricey botted water with a portable filtered bottle, at about 5c per bottle (Brita Fill & Go bottle is around $12, then refills every three months). Keep it in the fridge ready to go.

Savvy with computer programs? Another budgeting option is to use BudgetPulse.com, if you can export your banking data as a .QIF or .CSV. If you mainly use a Visa or cash card for spending, this way works. You may also use Pocketbook, which is a phone app and a quicker set-up. It also lets you know when regular bills are coming up, which is important for spending regulation.

In doing this, you'll need to determine basic categories of where money is spent into as few as possible... then it adds up the amounts under those categories. You'll probably be amazed at how much your monthly groceries actually cost!

Always try to buy furniture or whitegoods at wholesale outlets, op shops, or use trade discount cards – never pay retail on big items. I got a new queen sized, deluxe mattress for $250 delivered, just by spending an hour online finding the best deal.

What to do Before Buying Your First Property

If single, assess your lifestyle factors. It could be better making the purchase an affordable investment property, if you can continue to live happily in a shared rental apartment near your workplace.

If you can save a 20% house deposit, not only will it save on repayments, it will also mean you can escape the Lenders Mortgage Insurance fee of $5-7,000. (Some people ask their parents to guarantee the loan against their own house equity to avoid LMI; risky for the parents, not for the kids!)

Before you borrow, ensure your credit cards are at the minimum amount possible, not just the debt but the actual ceiling limit. This is because all borrowing limits are taken into account, along with any other loans. Pay out any personal loans.

Check your credit file at Equifax first, and then apply for a pre-approval letter from a mortgage broker or competitive lender. You want to know if there are any old bills about to ruin your lending chances before you make an offer on a house! Also be wary of identity theft, as that can make lending very difficult.

You are entitled to check your credit report for free once a year.

See https://www.mycreditfile.com.au or https://www.equifax.com.au/personal/corrections-portal

Finally, Create a Gap

The gap can also be thought of as positive cash flow. Since most wage earners spend 100% or even 110% of their income, it is important to *pay yourself first*: automatically direct transfer part of your income into a different account straight after you get paid. And don't use an EFTPOS card on the new savings account!

So many people rely on their memory or willpower to save, but this usually fails. Scratch that, it always fails.

Good financial management is not all about earning more, it's about spending less than you earn.

How Much to Save?

Using your budget planner and goals as a guide, plan to save or invest directly 10 to 15 percent of household income. This total includes voluntary superannuation (remembering it is not accessible), emergency cash, shares, managed funds, and paying down an investment property. It does not include Prada shoes.

If relying just on super for retirement, and you start at 45, you would need to sacrifice 30% of gross salary into super. Yikes!

If you struggle to save, consider depositing any family assistance lump sum or tax refunds into a high-earning savings account (online saver). This makes an ideal emergency fund that you may want to access within a day or two, but one you do not have an

EFTPOS card for. Some are tied to a transaction account, so bear in mind the wait while the transfer occurs.

A Rainy Day Account

A portion of your savings should be kept aside for emergencies.

What you want to provide for is just your 'bare bones' budget, in case of loss of income. If your living costs are $4,300 per month, but you could live on $3,500, then your emergency fund should be $10,000 or so, or three months' expenses. We had $20,000 in our offset account and this was used when our income stopped. It was a godsend.

Remember, the Government does not expect you to run a zero-income business and claim an unemployment allowance, as you need to be actively seeking fulltime work and go to interviews. Nor does the government pay Carers' Allowance if you provide temporary care for a sick or injured spouse (under 12 months).

Emergencies can be unforeseen repair bills, bereavement or sickness costs, surviving while a business income is faltering, redundancy, or one of you needing specialist medical attention. Some of these events can be insured against, e.g., private health insurance, income insurance. Even so, a lot falls outside insurance coverage.

Once used, this emergency account needs to be gradually replenished from your income after your life returns to normal.

It is a good idea to keep two to three months' living costs in an online saver account, for those unforeseen emergencies

If you are putting any extra money into your mortgage principal, this is great, but you also need to diversify. Living is risky business and you might not be able to access that growing equity in times of a crisis… unless you have a redraw facility. Look at building up investments that are tax effective, some with a shorter access time – referred to as liquidity.

Savings Goal Calculator

Go to: https://moneysmart.gov.au/saving

(See 'Savings Goal Calculator'). Try to save $1,000 first and build on that, reducing any personal debt in tandem. Also check out *Pocketbook* (Aus) or *GoodBudget* (global) mobile app for automatic budget tracking.

Note: It's financially dangerous to use a credit card facility for lifestyle expenses while out of work or for new business ideas.

Learning Points

* Look at ways to increase your income streams, through a hobby business or smart business marketing methods. It's also about reassessing your attitude to taking action.

* As your income rises, take stock and increase your regular savings amount (automated). Keep the gap between income and expenses.

* Plan to save / invest a portion of your income, if you don't currently have credit card debt.

* Keep a rainy day fund, with two to three months' worth of living costs at easy access.

* Find out where your money leaks are! Pen & paper people, keep a Spending Diary. Computer folks, buy almost everything with a debit card and upload all transactions to a budgeting mobile app or website budget planner.

Understanding Debt and Debt Reduction

Bad Debt

While the western world has generally reduced its spending on credit, many switching to using debit cards, North Americans owe $11.68 trillion, or $17,117 per debt holder[10], and Australians owe $33.9 billion, or $4,356 per debt holder.

Check with the MoneySmart calculator (https://moneysmart.gov.au/credit-cards/credit-card-calculator) to calculate what interest you really pay each year.

Certainly, we would all be better off without credit cards. But if you have got one or two, be mindful of the following:

* Do not accept limit increases. In fact, make the limit low enough to pay off in one month comfortably.

* If transferring card balances to lower interest payments, do not keep spending on the new card. Instead try to pay off what you owe within six months. Aim for a new credit card with a transfer interest rate of 0 to 2% for six months, and use those six months to pay it out, not to accrue more. If you don't pay it in that time, it will accrue a high level of interest, plus any new purchases will be at the full rate (check this rate).

---

7. http://www.nerdwallet.com/blog/credit-card-data/average-credit-card-debt-household/2014

* Store cards and "rewards" credit cards have much higher interest rates. If you do not usually pay the monthly balance in full, switch to a lower interest "no frills" card.

* Be aware that 55-day interest free periods are hard to achieve, since people often do not pay their statement in full, and on their next purchase the interest is accrued from day one. If you lower your limit to $500 or $1,000, you might be able to pay it out monthly and achieve 30 to 55 interest-free days.

* Any cash advances on credit cards are also charged at the full interest rate straightaway.

An alternative is to use a Debit Visa/Debit Mastercard. Banks, credit unions and building societies offer these cards for your everyday transaction account, with nil or low fees for use. It is used in the same way at the checkout as a credit card, except all the funds are yours.

Fees? There aren't few to none. I've found credit unions and building societies charge lower fees all-round for banking and most survey with higher customer satisfaction.

So that's credit cards taken care of, now what about those tempting pay-later offers on furniture?

Unless you are very disciplined and will pay within 12 months, *do not* take up "buy now with no deposit, no interest" schemes. These are notorious for letting consumers think they only have to make minimum repayments (they don't) and then when the free period expires, whacking them with up to 29% interest right back to the start of the loan, plus any default fees that might apply for non-payment. There is usually a set-up fee as well. Paying on lay-buy is a better option if available, or now we have Afterpay, which still means planning ahead logically for your payments.

Another point is that every credit card, store card, loan and hire purchase will count against your ability to borrow for a home loan, in the lender's eyes.

Saving While in Debt

Should you save, or pay off debt first? With paying off debt, you have a guaranteed return of the amount of your interest (perhaps 9% for home loans, or 20% for credit cards), and it also stops that interest compounding. With saving you may earn 7%, minus 2% in tax, so it is not as cost-saving as paying off debt. In the future your debt payments can instead become regular savings.

> *You will not be able to start active investing if you have large personal debts, so pay out the highest interest debts first.*

For those with major debt problems, consolidation of all personal loans and cards could be beneficial, if you find a low-interest loan or flexible mortgage facility. Instead of 17% or even 150%, you will be paying about 9% interest and manageable monthly payments. Then make a commitment to stop using credit.

Good Debt

Some people see all debt as bad, but there can be benefits of being in debt. Good debt is leveraging (borrowing) into assets to receive cash flow and/or an appreciating asset. When borrowing to invest and receive income, the interest is tax deductible, so the interest rate is not as big an issue as it is with your own home.

The leverage provided by borrowing is key to advancing your wealth. This is because you are earning income on the money you are borrowing, as well as making any growth on that money, thus enhancing the results. As your equity (the part you own) in property or shares grows, so too does your ability to borrow.

While many Australians fear getting into "too much debt", banks and other lenders only look at two things: security of your assets – with property top of their list – and ability to repay. Repayability depends entirely on total income (including yield, salaries, royalties, etc) being high enough and consistent.

Obviously it helps if there is another partner to pay too; but if you are single with medium to high income, then don't be discouraged. Rental counts as income (although only about 80% of total rent would be counted by most lenders). Share dividends count. Centrelink payments count. So even Pensioners are often able to borrow for investing purposes, if that asset generates good cash flow.

Types of Mortgages

Your own residential mortgage is not good debt, as it does not earn an income and is not tax-deductible. For this reason we are often advised to pay it off first (saving all that interest). Since any extra payments save you the current interest rate, free of tax, there is good argument for paying it down rather than saving separately.

This could be helped along with an **Offset account** that your salary goes into, as the balance in this side-by-side account is subtracted from the mortgage to get a smaller interest bill, and you can still use the cash as needed. If the loan states 100% offset, this means all funds in your cash account are working for you at the same interest rate as your loan, calculated on a daily basis. Any savings reduces your mortgage amount, while also being *non-taxable*. You could save for your child's education in here, as long as you don't envisage hardship when the child hits that time when you need to redraw it.

Similarly, with a **Line of Credit (LOC)** loan, the gap between what you earn and what you spend helps to pay off the loan. It is a pre-approved loan that you can use all at once, or a bit at a time. You can access paid-off equity easily while having access to your income for spending. Your fixed payment is interest only. These types of loans work well for disciplined investors and owners with at least 20 percent equity. Some have a fixed time frame, but many LOCs are revolving, allowing the lender to fund renovations or further property purchases without further approval (up to the original loan limit).

Another variation of this is an 'all-in-one' loan account, whereby all income goes into this account and all expenses come out. They offer direct credit of salaries and withdrawals via ATM, EFTPOS, linked credit card (no interest) or cheques. *The repayments are interest only*. Check the transaction fees, fee free limit, and monthly fees.

The downside: Since this works like a giant credit card, many people refinanced to these loans who are unused to budgeting do not make headway with their mortgages. (A considerable number do not realise how much they spend, and so lofty projections fail). As a LOC minimum requirement is interest only, it is up to you to ensure that more money is regularly transferred to pay off the principal.

Premium packaged loans (sometimes called wealth packages) are popular for investors borrowing over $125,000. For an annual fee between $240 and $490, you can benefit from a discount of 0.5–0.7% off the standard variable rate, a credit card fee waiver, and often no establishment fees to worry about. The flexibility of having all your banking needs in one package, able to be added to (without more loan fees) when buying more property, makes a packaged loan a good choice.

I recommend credit unions and other non-bank lenders with lower rates who don't charge annual fees, or if they do, it's still a great deal. There is a perceived risk when assessing lesser-known lenders, but it's not real – unless you start becoming a consistent loan defaulter of course.

Paying off your Home Loan Faster

While most people take out these flexible loans to pay off their home loans faster, it can prove too tempting. It was found in a survey by CPA Australia that "64% of people use a redraw, offset or all-in-one account to fund personal costs". Also, loans with extra features often have extra costs or higher interest than 'no frills' loans. So, it seems more important to know yourself and your goals when choosing the right home loan, than to simply have the most flexible loan.

> *"How can you save more in interest? By having your normal loan repayments halved or quartered, then deducted fortnightly or weekly, you achieve one extra repayment per year. (Or you can pay extra every month).*
>
> *I also recommend clients to base their repayments as if the interest rate were higher. So when rates do increase, this will not affect their lifestyle as they are already making the higher repayment. In one example, by manually calculating and increasing repayments to 1.25% above the actual rate, the long term savings are $160,479 in interest, reducing the 30-year term by 8.5 years."*
>
> *– James Sylvester, Your Home Loan consultant.*

What is Equity?

Equity is the difference between the value of the property and the loan balance. If you buy a good property and its equity reaches more than 25 percent of value, then your home equity can probably be used to purchase investment property, if your income is good and you don't already have many loans or credit cards. (These of course could be paid out first).

Note that you can only utilise 90 to 95 percent of this equity for lending, as lenders usually like to take a cautious approach.

Using Your Home Equity for Property Investment

So how can homeowners access their equity for investing? Say you've paid off quite a lot of the original loan; this is how a mortgage broker could structure it:

Example existing loan:

$500,000 - Property Value
<u>$350,000 - Loan Balance</u>
$150,000 - Total Equity

Increasing the loan to 90 percent of the property value ($450,000) will allow you to access an extra $100,000.

$500,000 - Property Value
$350,000 - Existing loan
$100,000 - New (second) loan

The interest paid on this new portion of the loan will be tax deductible if used to purchase an investment property, but you should organise a 'split account' to keep your principal home and investment property separate, according to mortgage broker, James Sylvester.

With your home purchase, time is on your side. In 20 years or so, the equity portion – from natural growth and repayments – should vastly outweigh your debt, and any mortgage still on it could be paid off with the sale of other assets.

While it's good to save on the huge interest cost, this debt devaluing makes paying down your mortgage fast, at great lifestyle sacrifice, a questionable idea. What else could you do with the extra funds, perhaps invest in a rental property?

For many people, paying off their home is their main focus, so here is a comparison of the two ideas.

Case Study: Paying off own House vs. Investing

John doesn't want to invest yet as feels the safer route is paying down his home mortgage fast. He bought a small house in the regions for $300,000 with a $280,000 mortgage. It averages 7 percent capital growth per annum. He only renovates once, spending $10,000.

John ploughs $800 extra per month into his home loan on top of normal repayments, so in 13 years, 6 months, he is debt free.

By Year 20, John has a house valued at $618,034 with no debt. Well done… but remember to consider inflation and debt deflation!

John's Goal: Pay Off House Quickly

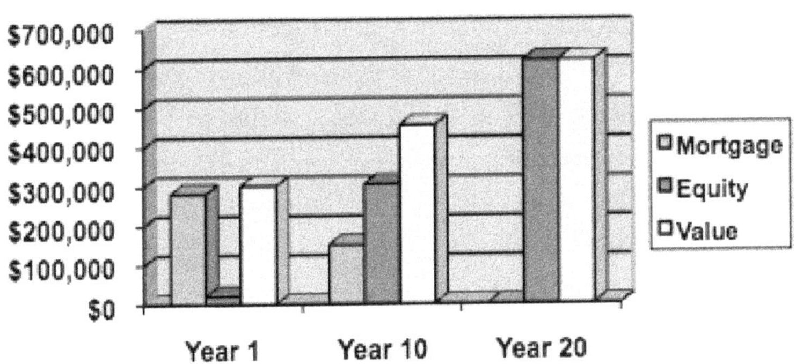

John is debt-free early, but he can now see that the sale of his home is only enough to buy a similar house that is no improvement in location, style, or size. Since John is now set to retire, he sees downsizing (buying a smaller home) as his only option to free up capital.

With most lenders you can borrow up to 80 or 90 percent of your home's value minus its debt (this is called an equity loan).

Now let's examine an alternative approach. His average-earning neighbour Jarrod bought for $300,000 also, but he would rather buy a property investment simultaneously and fund a small negative outflow per year, after all tax breaks. In year 3, with 25 percent equity, he can afford to invest in a $300,000 house around 15 kilometres from the CBD. It achieves 9 percent p.a. growth on average, as he chose wisely.

Since he must fund an investment, Jarrod pays his mortgage off rather slowly, leaving $90,000 owing after 20 years. His cash shortfall is initially $3,000 per year (decreasing annually), plus $30,000 for repairs and $25,000 in renovations over the 17 years. He also paid $15,000 in initial costs – funded by his existing equity (these costs will be excluded from CGT).

At year 20, his investment is worth $817,500. We'll pretend he did not pay any principal off this investment, so his equity is just $472,500. This adds to his principal place of residence equity of $618,034, giving Jarrod a gross equity of $1.1 million after 20 years.

Jarrod's Goal: Investing Excess Funds in Property

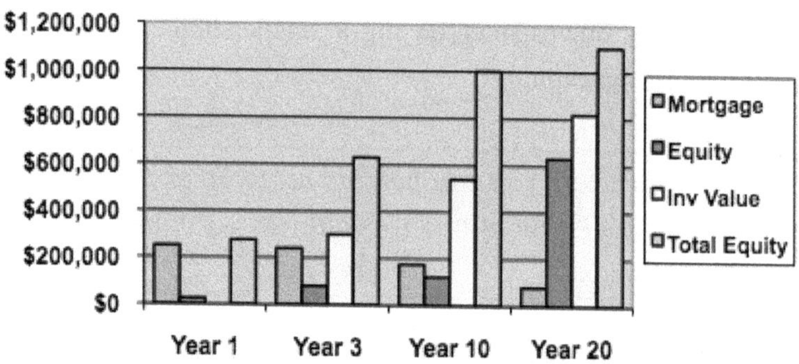

So, you can see that Jarrod used his legal tax deductions and natural capital growth to gain more equity overall. He actually put less money into his investment annually (about $5,735) than John did into his mortgage, so he could therefore pay the initial investing costs off, spread out over time.

What about Jarrod's mortgage? Say he chooses to pay off his own $90,000 mortgage by selling the investment. Upon selling, the capital gain amount is $500,000 – after improvements deducted from sale price, with the tax being $121,250 (50% of his marginal tax rate at say, 34%). After paying the real estate agent, he comes out with a profit of $376,750.

Adding this to his original home equity of $618,034, but minus the mortgage on his residence, Jarrod still beats John in this example after selling, with total equity or profit of $904,784.

This comparison is a conservative example based on just one investment. I have assumed that both these guys are ordinary wage earners with no special skills. Jarrod has put himself in front by directing his extra savings towards his investment rather than his own home. If his target was ten properties in 15 years, he could also potentially achieve that, with value-adding strategies and step-by-step financing.

Focussing on maximising capital growth definitely accrues a higher net worth faster, and this is imperative for many of us over 35 with no huge retirement fund.

Why is total equity so important? Because lending institutions will let you borrow money for any reason, even living expenses, if you have plenty of growing equity in secured assets and a regular income… from the rental yields, for example. (*See* 'Living Off Equity').

Lender's Mortgage Insurance: a Plus or a Minus?

On a standard mortgage, if borrowing more than 80 percent of the value of a property, you usually need to pay a Lenders Mortgage Insurance premium, which is a surety for the lender. It offers no mortgage protection for your benefit, but if you defaulted on the loan, then your lender gets paid by the insurer.

You can pay LMI either as one off lump sum at the establishment of the loan, or it can be capitalised onto the loan repayments.

Self-employed lenders often get caught when taking out 'low doc loans', as sometimes lenders require 60 percent LVR. Higher LMI premiums come along too. Lenders 'Aussie' and 'HomeLoans' currently offer low documentation loans with 80 percent LVR.

With a Mortgage-Secured Line of Credit loan, tapping into the equity in your existing home or having a family guarantee may allow you to borrow *up to 90 percent* of the value of a new investment property without paying LMI costs, since the excess is secured by your home equity. So shop around!

Because LMI is not portable, then consider the ramifications of paying a high premium (e.g. $10,000) that you may regret in 18 months' time when deciding to change lenders. If no equity has been paid down, you'd have to pay LMI again. LMI premiums on loans over $300,000 cost quite a lot more than those charged on loans less than $300,000.

Property Research

CoreLogic.com.au – Research & Reports

It's always good to know your local property market. See RP Data's free property analysis at https://www.propertyvalue.com.au.

This will tell you capital city median home values, growth rates, rents, gross yields, days to sell and discounting. They have a new tool which lets you match your strategy (capital gain, cash flow, or lower risk) to likely matching suburbs. You would need to upgrade to a premium subscription to find suited investments. Without getting too lost in it, look at two or three matching suburbs to your strategy.

HotSpotting... www.hotspotting.com.au – Research & Strategy

If you have a certain strategy that you're targeting, then Terry Ryder has the report for it. From 'Cheapies with Prospects', through to 'Capital Growth superstars' and 'National top 10 best buys', these paid reports outline the economic drivers, why invest there, and housing prices, all to match your strategy.

Learning Points:

* While bad debt in credit cards and store accounts can set us back in our financial lives, good debt (for assets) can help us get ahead if used wisely.

* Weigh up the pros and cons of investing in another property over a 20-year timeframe, rather than just paying down your own home mortgage fast.

* Learn about the ramifications of Lenders Mortgage Insurance before you go to buy property.

* Do research on the past growth, values and rental yields in at least a couple of suburbs before you invest in any one.

Basic Investing Strategies

Planning Your Way to Wealth

Once you have worked your way through all the investment options presented, and deduced which type of investments suit your risk profile (i.e. conservative, balanced or aggressive) and time horizon, then it is time to make your ***Financial Plan*** (see *Appendix*). Through the plan, you have an easy way of monitoring your overall financial situation every three to six months. Ideally it will trigger you to do more research and question all your investments' performances.

Now would be a great time to brush up on your basic money management knowledge. As I've said, MoneyMinded.com.au is a free online education program comprising eight topics. MoneyMinded was initiated and funded by ANZ Bank, with contributions from the community sector and education experts, including Financial Counselling Australia.

The Power of Compounding

Compounding is interest, earning interest. Your parent income (your capital) has children, their children also have children without any further effort on your part, so the value of the account grows at an ever-increasing rate, especially if it has a good rate of return.

There are three ways to aid compounding:

* Reinvesting dividends or other income

* Regular investing over time – called dollar cost averaging

* Holding your investment for a longer time span (and ensuring the best possible rate of return)

Compounding interest is referred to as "magic" because over time it can make a huge difference to wealth. An investment of $100 a month for 10 years at 5% yield will only net $15,500 at the end of the period, whereas $100 a month for 15 years at 10% yield would be worth $41,500. The extra time and the higher rate makes a huge difference. When saving for your child's future, these two factors are important.

'Buy and Hold' or 'Buy-Gain-Sell'?

No matter which asset class you have, a common problem is that many people think too short-term and concentrate only on trading for capital gain (the buy-gain-sell strategy). They try to pick the best vehicle for a quick ride to the top, which is near impossible to pick, followed by a whine about Capital Gains Tax on any profits when they sell. Many don't account for the transaction costs of such regular buying and selling, such as brokerage, entry fees, or stamp duties and real estate agent commissions. With the costs of property trading being so high, selling too soon or without pre-thought-out strategy could spell disaster.

There are some investors who make worthwhile profits from 'flipping' real estate, usually in the 'cheapies into beauties' property renovation industry. These investors really know how to budget their entire renovation and transactional costs though.

Patient investors using the 'buy and hold' strategy still have access to growth in most parts of the economic cycle, as they can borrow more off increased equity. They also reap all the benefits of ownership, including income if they choose.

Study the investors in the BRW 'Rich 200'. Were they trying to make a quick profit, or were they in it for the long haul, putting everything they had into their business or their investments? Long-term holders can invest for cash flow or for capital gain through reuse of equity.

Another advantage of buy and hold is: when investing in property over a long span of time there is little chance that you'll miss a boom period, so any lean years will be made up for with the flurry of growth in the few years of a boom. Since high capital growth properties are more likely to be negatively geared to begin with, the investor also gets the full tax benefits to enhance their wealth. Of course the investment must be affordable for you to hold through thick and thin.

You need to choose the right strategy for you. This could mean putting $300-400 cash per month into direct property while maximising tax deductions, to ensure a good cash flow in retirement. Or it could mean lending 50% to 60% against shares or funds you hold, for a long-term growth strategy.

Overall Diversification

First of all, the main reason people diversify into various asset classes is to spread the risk and allow at least one of their assets a chance to run. Because it's so difficult to pick the next winner, 'stayers' choose a sensible break-up of assets as part of their financial plan.

When investing, you should diversify away from your business or job. Many people have shares only in their company, and many a sorry tale comes out if the company folds.

Some real estate investors have all of their eggs in the residential property basket. Their theory is that diversification into other assets can dampen overall earnings and redirect much-needed funds. Generally these investors hold very large portfolios with stable incomes, so they can ride out any downturn in property.

Small investors do face larger risks. For instance, purchasing just one investment property, secured by your home, is a somewhat risky position. It's a bit like putting all your nest egg into your business and not having a sideline investment that can provide income. When you can afford to purchase other investments of any kind you will carry less risk. You would then have the flexibility of being able to sell a different class of investment, for example shares, to fund a shortfall that was brought on by an interest rate rise or bad tenant in your investment property, without having to sell that property in a flat or down market.

What makes up an ideal portfolio? It depends on your investor profile. A *Balanced* investor's strategy could be, after assessing the state of all asset classes, investing say 30% in property securities, 30% in Australian equities, 10% in global equities, 10% hedging strategies, 10% fixed interest, 5% private equity, and 5% in cash. This is an example of a large balanced portfolio under management.

Not everyone needs to diversify in every class, if they are financially educated 'active' investors. Work it out according to the present market conditions and forecasts, your goals and risk values. It is important to think of the probable future when thinking **asset allocation**, and not about what was hot last year.

Also, assess these choices in line with your tax and asset protection plan. Please see Chapter 16: *Protecting your Wealth* if you haven't got any asset protection plan!

Diversification within Share Investing

A commonsense approach is required regarding diversification. You must cull the losers and let the winners run in order to be in front at the end of the year.

You might still be wondering how many securities to buy. There is no point in buying small amounts of a huge number of stocks. It would take mighty good gains in the winners to compensate for the poor ones, plus you won't have time to research them that well. As a guide, in between three and ten varied stocks is enough. But what matters more than quantity, is the quality of these stocks.

Diversifying between **speculative stocks** in different sectors is pointless, as the risk is still high. In fact, for novices speculative buying is a minefield.

Similarly, there is no point to sell good **blue chip stock** to enter into a riskier investment with a small company, just to re-weight your portfolio. Re-weighting is often advised when one stock becomes larger in value than all the others in your portfolio. A stockbroker might say "you're heavy in resources, you better get this new biotech company". Don't listen to them! Look at the underlying value of the company in question before making any decisions.

Diversification within Managed Funds

Diversifying in Managed Funds is not just holding three funds with the same manager (i.e. AMP), it is spreading investments over different managers with different philosophies. Their focus can be broken down into "income" (investing for dividends) or "growth" (investing for capital gain). You can also diversify into different sectors within a single fund, e.g. Australian equities, international equities, property securities, fixed interest, etc. This strategy is useful if you are not quite sure which market is going to perform best in the short to medium term.

Dollar Cost Averaging

Dollar cost averaging is another secret of investing. This means you buy either shares or units in funds at regular intervals. By paying the average market price, you cannot pay "too much" over time. It means you're buying less when prices are high, and more when they're lower. There's no guesswork involved in picking 'bottoms' or 'tops'. Depending on the fund, you can contribute from a minimum of $100 or $200 per month by automatic direct debit.

Dollar Cost Averaging will mean you buy less when prices are high, and more when prices are lower.

Learning Points

* Ensure you are using compounding effectively by reinvesting dividends or paid interest.

* The 'buy and hold' method of investing does allow tapping of equity – it's all in how the loans are structured.

* Consider all the costs of purchasing, renovating, and selling your investment, including tax implications.

* Because of the cyclical nature of markets; you need to diversify your investments. Start slowly, yet try to spread your risk both over asset classes and within asset classes.

Choosing a Broker

It is often necessary to deal with business brokers, mortgage brokers, stockbrokers, real estate agents or buyers agents, once you decide to invest. So use a company that caters for investors, and ask if the broker is also an active investor.

For home loans, are you better off going to a mortgage broker or deal direct with the lender? The advantages of a broker include:

* Saving you time and many calculations,

* Independent ones may assist you in avoiding exit fees, and

* Some brokers may help push a loan through, due to their lender knowledge.

Disadvantages are: you might end up paying more for your loan if they aren't independent, you could be charged high fees, they may advise you to borrow more than you need, and refinancing needlessly could be costly for your equity.

If you want to ease your paperwork and running around burden, find a good mortgage broker that suits your purpose. Ensure that they have a wide range of bank and non-bank lenders on their books, so that you are not limiting your choices. And check that they are registered with the Mortgage Industry Association: www.miaa.com.au.

Stockbrokers and Online Brokers

Traditional stockbrokers give advice and earn their commissions from customers buying and selling. They are reticent to advise you to sell unless to buy something else, because they make more money having your money active in the market. But how do investors make money? Through holding stock of good companies, and selling rarely. Chopping and changing a lot does eat away at your funds, because of brokerage fees and selling at the wrong time.

These days you're in the driver's seat: you can choose to be advised by a full service broker and pay a premium, or you can research and choose stocks yourself with the help of a discount broker. Take a look at CommSec's "What to Know before Investing in Shares" guide:

https://bit.ly/Commsecguide

There are some brokers with an online broking price, while others provide information with their broking (called a "full fee" stockbroker). You can also discover about margin lending, buying warrants or options, where to buy shares and managed funds, and simulating geared versus normal buying.

Ultimately, you decide which company to buy or sell for a low fixed price per time. For CommSec discounted share trading (brokerage from $10), you open a Commonwealth Trading Account with a minimum of $500, which you then use as your base account to trade with. The best priced brokerage is for those with a CDIA account, which has no fees. CommSec houses free research and *stop loss* or *watchlist* tools that are very useful.

At a lower entry point, the app 'CommSec Pocket' allows investors to start trading (via ETFs) from as little as $50 and $2 a trade. Sharesies is similar; you can buy shares or ETFs and part-shares, from as little as $50, with fees of .50c to $2.49 per trade. (Sharesies.com.au).

CommSec and InvestSMART also rebate most entry fees as units if you buy managed funds through them. Saves up to 4% entry fee! InvestSMART also have a TrailCap program where their trailing commissions are capped at $396 p.a., and of any further commissions, 50% are rebated to you the customer.

Once you get used to looking up share prices, company news, price charts (comparing performance on-screen with the All Ordinaries Index), EPS, DPS, yield and forecasts, you will feel more in control of your investing. You could say this research is step one of "active investing". You do not need special software for this real-time information; all that you need is available for customers at the online discount brokers.

Only people classed as regular traders might need special charting and share monitoring software to more readily assess their trades.

What about Trading Systems?

There are many trading systems for foreign exchange or share trading, often relating to day traders. They are appealing to the 'get rich quick' mentality.

Buyers Agents

If you're searching for a property to buy in another State, or you want to take the emotion and research time out of an investment purchase, a buyer's agent can be worthwhile. There is no minimum buy price, but the average agent charges around 1.5 to 3% + GST of property value for a full buying service. If you simply require them to negotiate a property price before, during or after an auction, typical agent fees are set at 1% + GST of total purchase price (or a pre-agreed fixed fee).

Find a buyers agent at the Real Estate Buyers Agents of Australia http://rebaa.com.au.

Learning Points

* Mortgage brokers might help you to save time and find a way through the lending maze, but check their registration and fees.

* Realise that stockbrokers want you to trade actively, but this can cost you many buy/sell fees and sometimes profits.

* Online discount brokers can save you lots of fees and provide customers with in-depth market and company analysis. The only downside is it makes it easier to pull the trigger too often.

A Retirement Nest Egg

With people living longer, we are all going to need a lot more money than we imagine. Many have disruptions to working life (like having babies), so just compulsory super is probably not enough to cover the many years we might survive.

"How much will I need?" is the catchcry. That all depends on your needs and expectations: do you want to live on a lesser salary than what you are used to, such as 50%? Do you think that your retirement fund's returns will keep in front of inflation? Would you like a private nurse? Is a life-saving operation going to cripple you financially? What about travelling?

Financial advisers might suggest that you are going to need $1 million to retire on for 25 years. This is to spur you to plough more into super and managed funds. Of course it is up to you. You may want to strike the fine balance of living well now but sacrificing a small amount to Super/Retirement Savings, so that you can live without hardship later. The tax-effectiveness of such salary sacrificing also makes it better than saving long term outside of super.

The *Association of Superannuation Funds of Australia* believes for those wanting to live a **comfortable** retirement, a single person needs an annual income of $45,962 or a couple needs $64,771 (2021). Couples seeking a 'modest' retirement lifestyle need to spend $41,929 a year, while singles would need $29,139 to keep a modest lifestyle. Every single year, this rises again.

If you want the usual ability to buy furniture, private health insurance, a reasonable car, good clothes, a range of electronic equipment, and domestic and occasionally international holiday travel, then aim for at least the *comfortable* retirement level.

Varying amounts up to $700,000 are needed for this current target, depending on retirement age (and age you are going to live to!)

Check how long your own money will last with the range of super calculators at www.sunsuper.com.au (retirement modeller).

Super-Boosting! If, as a resident, you earn under $41,112 in a year, the Low-Income Super Contribution kicks in 50 cents in every dollar of any after-tax super contributions made, up to $500. If earning under $37,000, you may also receive a low income super tax offset automatically, on any amounts you contribute.

So, if you run your own business, it's time to contribute your 10 percent (after costs of course).

What about the Age Pension?

If you are near retiring age and you can live on $987 a fortnight (singles) or $744 a fortnight for couples (Australia: 2022), then read no further. I noticed this amount has barely gone up in the past decade, compared to the cost of living.

Indeed, relying solely on the Pension in the future may not be viable; a part pension is more probable. The sheer number of baby boomers retiring will mean miserly Government pensions continue… as well as extending the 'retirement age' up to 67, 70, etc. Those unprepared may need to delay retirement and work on, yet there is no need to have your financial life dictated by Government decree!

The Pension Bonus Scheme – for over-65s who keep working – is now closed to new applicants. Recent changes to pensions, pension ages, and superannuation pave the way for the Federal Government's grand plan for us all: *self-funded retirement.*

Divorcing?

Someone coming out of divorce should plan for a retirement that is self-sustaining and be careful with investing their divorce settlement.

Taking into account all the costs of home ownership is important for anyone just separated. Women often elect to keep the family home but without as much income, it can be hard. Similarly, you don't want to carry lots of heavy mortgage debt into your 60s, when downsizing might be a better option.

Reassessing the future of any joint investments is also imperative. Regardless of the year of divorce, Capital Gains Tax is assessed on the purchase price of any investment property – and the one who ends up owning it will have to pay it. On the upside, finding a 'nest egg' strategy based on personal goals is often easier to determine than a joint strategy.

Creating Your Own Pension

Forget term-allocated and allocated pensions, they have been superseded by account-based pensions. These pensions are most appropriate for good earners aged from 55s to 60s whom are salary sacrificing, as it provides a tax-free environ to build wealth. But others with Super fund nest eggs can also secure one.

How it works is: your traditional fund accumulates super while the pension fund runs alongside, earning good returns. Earnings in the account-based pension remain tax-free.

The nature of these pension accounts means some offer ATM access and other bank-type services. While the minimum annual drawdowns start from just 4% (for those aged 55-64) and 5% for 65-74, there is a danger of withdrawing too much of your nest egg from accessible pension accounts. For this reason, on retiring you need a written plan and know what annual limits you can withdraw before (a) age pension cuts out, and (b) your capital is depleted too much for future years. Super fund financial advisers can help you with planning and by law they must make it clear to you.

See *Chapter 14: What About Super?* for more on income streams and pensions.

Rising Cost of Living

It seems clear that the cost of living is going to rise dramatically, with droughts and fewer oil resources having deep impacts on groceries, water, petrol and transport costs. Already we are seeing a rise in food costs. Health costs and health insurance continue to spiral upwards every year. Truly, I am not trying to make you depressed!

I firmly believe everyone can create their own goals unhindered by Government rules, for example, to have an income stream of $80,000 per year. I suggest such high goals because you never know what is around the corner for you and your family. Why settle for retiring on half of what you now earn?

Did you ever think water would cost $3 or $4 a bottle when you were ten years old? When I was that age, potato chips at the corner dairy cost 25c, and water was free.

Living Off Equity

With an equity access loan, the lender lets you borrow up to 80% of the appraised value of your property. This type of financing lets you borrow for property or share investing, even including the one-off costs and deposit, if you have enough equity.

Also, lending against your existing property may allow you to borrow more than 80 per cent (up to 90 per cent) of the securing property's value. The payment of Lenders Mortgage Insurance (LMI) in this case depends on the lender's terms. So shop around!

With reverse mortgages (equity release), retirees are actually living off the equity in their home by borrowing a lump sum or monthly amounts… and deferring the compounding interest on the mortgage until they sell or pass away. They do not need to make repayments. This idea may sound scary for homeowners, indeed it is, if all equity is used up for lifestyle before you die! A large buffer of equity and a steadily growing property value is required for this to work.

Instead, imagine you are near retirement and have acquired five properties about nine years ago that are now valued at a total of $2 million (today's dollars). You have been negative gearing, with no repayments, on 'interest only' loans. There is now equity of $1 million. At an 8% averaged annual growth, pre-tax gain on equity at this point is $80,000, while the whole portfolio gains $160,000 – but you cannot access that much. Pay costs and shortfalls, receive rent, and you are gaining about $110,000 clear per year… on paper at least.

This changes when the houses become cash-flow positive, at which time you can access (for true lending) up to 80% of the entire gain, whittling out a bit for your living costs. So, many investors work towards 'owning' more than 50% of their properties before they retire, at which point the lender will let you eat up some equity in a draw-down (some call it a revolving line of credit). Since this method is tax-free, you will need less 'salary' than usual. It only works if the market remains in growth.

One problem with living off equity lies in financing: the major lenders have a problem with debt-servicing ratios for people with no other income. If you acquire plenty of rental income then this is not a problem. You might also get around this by using "low doc" line of credit loans. This strategy involves work to set up, and an active management style. Refinancing all properties at maximum value every few years is also necessary, but the results are well worth it.

You are working towards either paying them off or selling out. And your main residence is still there for future generations. If this appeals but you need financing help, you would do well to find a finance strategist/mortgage broker with expertise in this area.

A Line of Credit loan is a good tool for the savvy property investor. It allows you to keep re-using the loan without filling out applications, as you can reuse the original loan amount for borrowing again, if it is enough. Ensure your investment loan and main residence home loan are two separate accounts or sub-accounts, so that your tax-deductible costs are not mixed up with non-deductible expenses (a nightmare for any accountant).

Some financial advisers recommend borrowing with an increased Line of Credit home loan to buy shares and managed funds, but you'd be crazy to risk paid-off equity for anything less than a diversified and risk-averse portfolio. Also check the fees on managed funds and aim for low-fee funds. (You might find it easier to find these yourself, than relying on a particular financial planner).

Learning Points

* To determine what you need for retirement, think about what kind of retirement lifestyle you desire and the income needed to achieve this.

* Look at what the retirement modelling calculator says about your present superannuation commitment and adjust as needed. Avoid being depressed by paying in a bit more.

* Living off equity means relying on ongoing property growth… and it also means paying down debt quite efficiently. How determined and disciplined can you be?

Choosing the Right Wealth Vehicle

Spotting "the Next Big Thing"

It is a common fallacy that you can make big money merely by spotting "the next big thing", or area to invest. There is a little more to it. Nevertheless, it pays to be watchful of markets in the major asset classes. By reading the investor news and looking at the Economic Clock, we can find out which is having its day in the sun this year, and which – if certain economic criteria are met – could appreciate the best next year.

A lot of Australia's market movements are triggered by what is happening in the US. Things to watch are inflation increasing, interest rate hikes (and rumours of it), and how the large corporations are doing.

The other economy driving world markets is China, with India and other developing nations hot on its heels.

Becoming aware of the economic cycle will help you to spot upcoming booms and slumps.

We must ask ourselves: "is the market good value? To assess this, you need to watch inflation, interest rates, P/E ratios and earnings growth, commodity prices (if interested in resources sector), exports, and hot political topics and its effects. Phew!

Good value depends more on the earnings of companies rising steadily, not on how much money is ploughed into the general sharemarket.

Remember to get your share trading and market trend information from the ASX, Commsec or Bloomberg, not from the neighbour or an unlicensed advisor.

Following the Market Cycle

The crowd is always late, hopping on the bandwagon as they see others climbing aboard. This human tendency is known as market sentiment. *Counter-cyclical investing* just means investing opposite to the market sentiment, being a 'contrarian'.

Remember, most of your friends (and agents) will be wrong about the right time to buy. They will tell you to get in too late, when the market has already made its grand move!

Before investing, you should know where we are in the economic cycle. What are people talking about in the Press and on the street? The "Economic Clock" (created circa 1900) helps us see which part of the economic cycle we are in. The top of the clock is Boom, while the bottom is Slump.

Studying the clock, we become aware that these market changes are cyclical and inevitable. The Australian economic cycle traditionally lasts between 7 to 10 years, with a longer bull or bear market as well, but watch out for property cycles, which move faster than this at times.

Remember to also focus on the mood that the market creates and being wary of this.

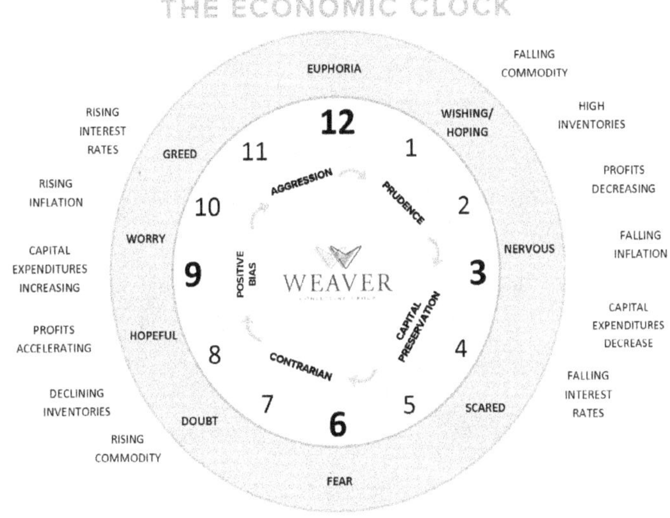

Clock with emotions. Source: WeaverConsultingGroup.com

No boom can last more than a few years

As interest rates hit rock bottom, defensive (fixed interest) investors look for better returns. With a need for stability, some might seek low-maintenance property. Others with an eye on the swelling house values also invest. This pushes the property market higher. At about the same time or after this, institutional and private investors pile into the sharemarket and traded funds. But gradually, as inflation eats away and lending rules tighten, the roar of the market flow becomes a trickle.

As our sharemarket becomes overvalued and falters, there are a lot of investors who withdraw to cash, crypto or gold. Some consider direct property investing, while high net worth folk might use portfolio hedging strategies and look to overseas.

Property Booms

In Australia, the property market is segmented, and each capital city is in a different part of the cycle. For those following a capital growth strategy, look for good locations where property has only *started* to rise (say 5% growth in previous year), after about two years of flat or negative growth. This will prevent you buying at the top, just before a bust period (normally lasting one to two years straight after a boom).

Try to think of interest rate rises not as a problem but as an opportunity. When interest rates are low, investors naturally tend to buy property in hot spots. This activity pushes up the house prices in capital cities like Sydney and Melbourne, and at times, Perth and Brisbane.

When there are *increasing* interest rates and higher debt levels, some investors will find home loans too expensive and have to sell. First home buyers tend to suffer mortgage stress more in a rising interest market. With more forced sales, investors can pick up bargain housing in locations that show solid long-term growth and planned infrastructure improvements. Buying in these times is counter-cyclical investing in action, with a view to long-term profitability. Of course, ensure the purchase is also affordable for your budget.

While you should definitely avoid buying in a boom, if taking a long-term approach to property, precisely timing the property market is not imperative. Your success depends on buying the right kind of property *for you*, with a manageable cash flow and comfortable debt level across all loans.

> *"When buying a property for investment, one consideration is you generally cannot buy or sell part of a property (it's either all or nothing) whereas you can sell part of a share portfolio" – Charles Beealerts with Kevin Forde (in 'Understanding Investments')*

In many of our major cities, demand exceeds supply when vacancies are lower than 1.5%. Australia is so varied with property cycles; most capital cities are at a different point in the cycle (e.g. upswing, recovery, or boom). If you've missed the boat in your area, you'll only have to travel a bit to find fundamentally solid property (good location, desired type of property, fair price) at the time when it suits your circumstances. It's also possible to invest overseas for better yields, with the aid of a cross-border tax accountant. (Try not to get swayed by a seminar).

Buying off the plan?

It's very hard to time markets to a tee. Buying off the plan can be folly, since many small housing developments pop up in a boom, but by the time the units sell the local unit market is returning to normal prices or is oversupplied. The price you locked in two years ago would then be too high for the market and you may have to sell at a loss. (Some people move in themselves, to wait for a better time to sell).

Do Your Homework

Reading a variety of good media sources will key you in to what is driving the markets and possible areas that are set for growth. This may only take a couple of hours per week if you scan the media.

Watch ABC's nightly market news (Alan Kohler), perhaps read Investor/Business sections of the major newspapers, subscribe to an investing magazine (*Money* or AFR *Smart Investor*) and a general money newsletter. The magazines are particularly insightful and current.

Investor forums are also interesting for keeping up with what investors think, although nothing to base your selection on.

Share Café: https://boards.sharecafe.com.au/
Aussie Stock: https://www.aussiestockforums.com/forums/
YNAB: https://support.youneedabudget.com/
MoneySmart: https://moneysmart.gov.au/#grow-my-wealth

The worst places to get your market information are from friends, relatives, and private trading or 'wealth creation (buy our product)' seminars. Some educational courses on the other hand, can form a vital part of your learning, so ensure the course or seminar provider is a proven, qualified educator.

Another thing to be wary of is, in the sharemarket, rumour rules. The 'smart money' (the wealthy and the fund managers) will make share prices move up as they invest, and it is this movement you must be alert to in order to invest early enough to profit, if growth is your goal. Yet research the fundamentals too. The actual company announcements are too late for any savvy investor, and often come accompanied by a dip in share price. Once the media start writing long articles on how company X is booming, and taxi drivers are recommending it, you've probably missed the boat.

Don't rely on news journalists for particular 'stock' buys.

A quick way to keep abreast of reliable investment opinion is by reading a finance commentator's column or blog. Respected Australian finance commentators:

Alan Kohler (ABC News, Inside Business, BusinessSpectator.com.au, Eureka Report, alankohler.com)

Scott Pape (Triple M radio, Barefoot Investor)

Marcus Padley (The Age, SMH, ABC TV's Inside Business, crikey.com)

Michael Pascoe (newspapers, radio) and

David Koch (Sunrise, Money Matters).

Spending this time researching, you will learn much about the realities of finance along the way. Before plunging in, you must assess all possibilities in line with your time horizon and attitude to risk.

Learning Points

* Studying the economic clock helps us realise that market moves are cyclical and inevitable.

* Buying in a down part of the cycle, when interest rates are rising and restricting many, is counter-cyclical investing in action.

* Ensuring a manageable cash flow and debt level for you long-term is likely more important than buying at the very lowest point in the cycle.

Property Vs. Shares Debate

Over the years we've seen experts debating property vs. shares, usually expounding that their industry gave the best growth. In this simplified viewpoint, over an 88-year view, shares on the All Ordinaries Index come out in front at 11.5% p.a. average growth, compared to 11.1% p.a. for residential property (including rental yields and 2% costs). At times in the economic cycle, one could be better off with shares, and at other times, with property.

This type of argument misses several vital points. Investing in direct shares (without gearing), novice Mums and Dads only make money in **two main ways**, that is: distribution income that is usually tax-paid already (3-5% is typical), and capital growth. We call 100% tax-paid dividends fully franked. Sure, these two ways can be enough, but many of us fail to capitalise because it's so easy to sell shares after hearing media hype or private investor rumours.

Leverage is through borrowing, but novice investors may fear gearing into shares. This is due to the risk of margin calls. If you prefer, this risk can be lowered with a lower gearing ratio, such as 50% or less. Good research also lowers your risk.

With direct property, novice investors can make money in at least **three ways**, with four benefits:

1. Through rental income, i.e. positive cash-flow
2. Through capital growth, boosted by leveraging

3. Through improvements to the property that lead to an increase in official value (after all costs)
4. Tax deductions from the investor's salary also make it much more affordable to hold.

The other reasons that ordinary Australians love property investment are: familiarity with it, tangibility, lifestyle reasons, and the historical proof that residential property in Australia grows well in value.

It is illiquid though, meaning it takes time to sell, and you must sell the whole house, whereas with shares you can sell a few and keep the rest. You can easily add more of your savings to shares for a cost of $20, while with property the way to add value is through smart renovations, which is a little harder for most of us.

Why Love Leverage?

Wealth is achieved faster with property if you're highly geared and achieve good capital growth. The maximum ratio of borrowing to assets is around 65% in shares and managed funds, compared to a maximum ratio of about 90% in investment property. This means investment property can be more highly leveraged, which makes a difference to your growth of wealth, as illustrated below. (It also adds to your overall risk however).

The power of leverage can be demonstrated with the simple example below. We start with capital or equity of $20,000. Considering upfront costs, what amount will you have at the end of year 1 if you chose ordinary shares, shares with 50% gearing, or a $200,000 townhouse with 90% gearing?

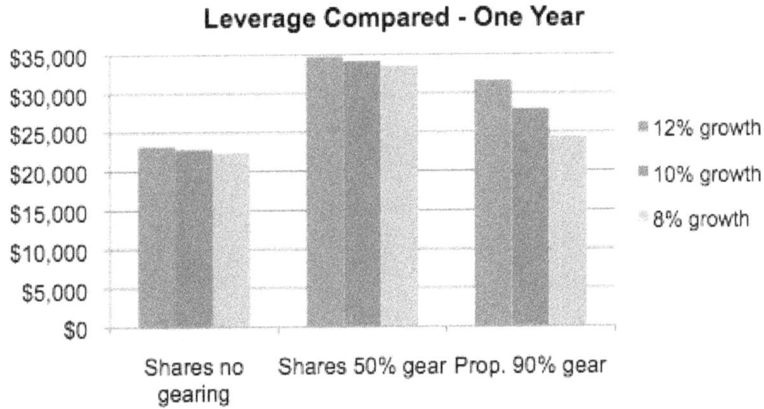

Notes: Assumes shares earn 4% yield and dividends are reinvested. Cash-flow shortage is not taken into account on property comparison but nor are rental yields. Assumes property costs $10,000 in fees and Govt. duties upfront. Gearing analysis does not take into account interest payments and tax benefits.

The amount you'd still have in Shares earning 4% net, at 12% growth and 50% gearing is $34,700. While at the end of one year, Property at 12% growth and 90% gearing leaves you with $31,600 – because $10,000 was eaten up in fees and costs.

Yet the differences expand when compared over time, as we see in the ten-year chart below. Investors need more time in the property market to counteract the high upfront costs and come into the right phase of the market.

Note: Be careful that this projection is not too high for your intended location of investment. Check growth predictions with Residex or Corelogic information.

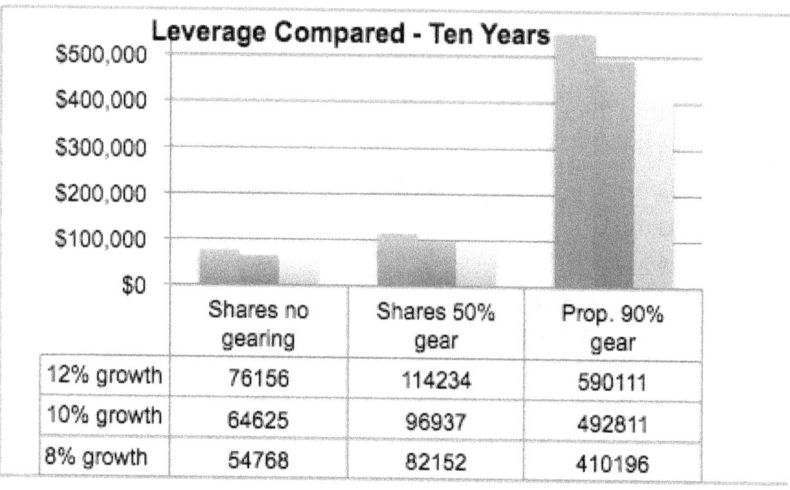

	Shares no gearing	Shares 50% gear	Prop. 90% gear
12% growth	76156	114234	590111
10% growth	64625	96937	492811
8% growth	54768	82152	410196

This chart assumes 4% yield on shares, growth at the rate stated, and minus $10,000 yearly in out-of-pocket costs of holding the property.

This kind of potential growth is why many investors are prepared to put up with negative cash-flow for a while.

Another hard-to-grasp concept is that while shares fluctuate daily, property values also rise and fall without our knowing it. Some years property will decline or stagnate, another year it may rise by 22% in a boom. So, timing of your purchase will affect your results.

Those in property sales like to quote that house prices double every 7-10 years but this depends on where you invested and when you invested. If Brisbane metro has only grown an average of 7% over ten years, mainly all it once, then it might not be wise to assume you're going to get the capital growth as on the chart above.

The slowdown mentioned above seems inevitable, particularly as Australia has become one of the most unaffordable places for housing in the world.

If you are still wondering whether to invest for capital gain or cash flow in residential property, it depends whether your goal is to grow your net wealth or to grow a nice little income pie. Generally, high growth is found in Australia's capital cities (particularly Melbourne/Sydney), and positive cash flow is more likely in country regions or in alternatives like student accommodation.

These days it makes sense to be cautious and invest within your range of holding affordability. You can help along returns with diligent buying and tightly budgeted renovations.

What are the Downsides of Property Investing?

Ordinary people get carried away during boom phases, buying off the plan, speculating on overstated profits, and taking on high levels of debt in regards to their income. Hence they become stuck with an over-valued property they can ill afford. Another trap is getting caught up in emotions when viewing something you like, such as a holiday unit in a beach suburb you enjoyed, instead of using your head, doing local research and crunching the numbers. You could be left with an unaffordable money pit.

Whether buying property or shares, identifying which part of the economic cycle we are currently experiencing is vital… so that you do not buy at the top of the market. In booms, real estate developers will advise newcomers to buy a new property "as you can't lose". Don't fool yourself – if it's got their $40,000 commission on top, you will lose out when it comes time to sell or revalue.

Not only that, new properties already have a premium price tag that will lose value over time. A-ha, building depreciation allowance is given for a reason.

Another thing to consider is the lack of diversity when starting out. As the cost of getting into multiple properties is high, and financing potentially difficult, shares and funds do offer an easier way to diversify risk.

Offsetting this is the consistent growth trend that residential property has shown from the 1970s to 2007, with investors less likely to chop and change. So when all factors are weighed, perhaps property is not such a high risk in return for the hefty rewards provided by leveraging. However, it is not the type of investment you can dip into for a year and come out in front.

Decrease Risk Through Buffers

As property is illiquid (it sells slowly), astute investors keep a line-of-credit buffer or cash account, so that they can take advantage of good opportunities quickly or make up the shortfall if there are vacancies.

A line-of-credit buffer is the gap kept between what is owed and the original limit on the investor's loan (perhaps for their primary residence). Thus the paid-off portion of a revolving Line of Credit loan can be drawn down by the owner at any time; allowing him/her to renovate, pay a deposit, or pay for large unforeseen costs. A cash buffer is even more flexible, and can save the investor's bacon when in a personal financial crisis or a high interest rate period.

Add a 2% interest-rate-rise buffer when calculating your mortgage affordability, to keep you from getting into hot water

---

To conclude, while property investing offers less diversity and more up-front costs, the rewards of owning strong capital growth properties over time (at least a cycle) have made many Australians wealthy.

Learning Points

* Determine whether you want to grow your overall wealth, or achieve a nice income pie.

* Invest within your range of holding affordability. You can help along returns with diligent buying and tightly budgeted renovations.

* With property, growth in wealth over ten years is much better than over one year, and this is because of the high costs of entry and greater leverage.

* Keep a line-of-credit buffer or cash account, in case you need to make up shortfalls when a tenant leaves, renovate, or pay a deposit.

* Risks can be managed by using equity or cash buffers, doing your due diligence (such as building and pest inspections and comparisons with similar properties), and getting landlords and building insurances.

Shares: What to Look for

Nothing is for certain in the markets. The unpredictability of share markets is best explained by economist, Burton G Malkiel. In *A Random Walk Down Wall Street*, Malkiel states: "a random walk is one in which future steps or directions cannot be predicted on the basis of past actions." This means that short-term price changes cannot be foreseen. And predicting the bottom of the market is darn near impossible.

To develop a trading system, you will need to focus on your objectives (for fun or for profit?), your technique for stock picking, timing, and the amount of loss you are prepared to wear before you say, stop!

The Australian *All Ordinaries Index* is not a leading index, but our economy is set to be the 12th strongest in the world. IMF (International Monetary Fund) predicts 4% growth in GDP in 2022. The All Ords offers a great assortment, some with high price volatility (like media and bio-tech stocks), and others with steady growth and yields (like Woolworths / CBA).

If investing long term, always look for a selection of stocks that offer good steady income (franked dividends), and look into large, quality leaders in their sectors. With the trading research tools provided at online brokers, you can also see if there were any "earnings surprises" in the stock's past. Look for negative earnings and also for any recent negative press concerning their outlook.

You may be tempted to invest mainly in a company you see is doing well within your field of expertise. Without knowing the major fundamentals (like management expertise and future earnings) of the company and why it is currently riding high, it is a risky endeavour. Once you know it is solid, then it could be a good buy for part of your portfolio (not more than 15%).

To make capital gains, seek currently undervalued companies; that is, solid companies with good management and financials that are currently out of favour with the investor market. They may have a low P/E ratio but rising earnings. Look at Harvey Norman Holdings as an example. At times the large retailer/landlord goes out of favour with investors, but the company itself keeps on building value. Dulux has been building value too.

Don't buy merely on a price drop; that could be a response to a bad earnings announcement, a rumour, or merely a sign some investors are taking their profits. In fact, there is a theory that investing in large cap stocks who have had the best one-year price growth actually works better.

Use the ASX (www.asx.com.au) website to look up share prices, announcements, charting and market information.

Which Stock Picking Method?

Which method are you going to choose your stocks with?

Fundamental analysis is the most common, involving looking at a company's earnings, prospects, and management.

First, check that your preference has a sustainable competitive advantage – perhaps it is the best-known brand name or it is in a monopoly environment.

Then look at the potential market size of the company – local or global? You can see by the up-and-down nature of resource stocks that global demand for iron ore or coal plays a role.

Also look at company size and track record. Larger companies that have been around longer are normally considered less risky, so they command a premium price.

Is the firm a potential takeover target? Mergers and acquisitions often increase the value of the stock.

Technical analysis is another strategy, whereby analysts look at the share price charts and assess whether to buy based on price patterns. This involves close analysis of price trends. There is a whole language which chartists use, such as "retracement", "support zone", "break out", etc, so it takes a bit of study to understand.

Downsides of Online Share Trading

With the speed and availability of online investing, it has encouraged a new breed of short-term traders. The price ups and downs displayed minutes after trading, and ability to speculate with options, CFDs, warrants, etc, tends to encourage even normally conservative people to 'play the market'.

If you want a thrill from trading, try a sharemarket game instead (at the ASX), where you don't risk your hard-earned cash on a gamble.

Time and again, it has been proven that holding a **blue chip** stock long term is more profitable than buying and selling in an attempt to make quick profits. Better yet, novices are better to pool their funds in an ETF, LIC or other managed fund which itself invests in a selection of blue chips, also traded on the stock exchange.

The upside of investing with Online trading brokers such as CommSec is you can use Conditional Orders, watchlists, and SMS alerts. You can set an order to buy on a rising price, a falling price, or sell either way. Ensure that when using this buying method that you can transfer enough cash to the trading account within three days, the average settlement period.

Don't Run With the Herd

In February 2007 the Shanghai stock market had a small plunge of 8%, not even noted by reporters at the time, which led the European, American and Australian markets into a freefall. Those close to the market overreacted to the Shanghai news. Local traders who were panicked by the fall on international markets were just swept up in "the herd mentality", while investors that were waiting to buy saw that dip as a chance to secure some shares they wanted at a better value, since they knew that it did not reflect the strong Chinese economy. (*Source:* Michael Pascoe, Yahoo7 *Money Matters, Feb 28 2007*).

Varieties of this situation happen regularly in our sharemarket.

When you have your money on the line, it is very hard not to become caught up in the emotions of either greed or fear. Speculation fuels price rises, while rapid price drops coax investors to snap up a 'bargain'. But the drop could be the start of a long downturn for the company share. Novices would do better to buy a little every month or so (called *dollar cost averaging*) than buying all at once and mistiming the market. Remember, if the basic fundamentals of the market do not change, keep a cool head. If you hear a stock buy tip, just ignore it.

Two things drive markets and are enemies of profit:
***Greed** and **Fear**.*

Stopping the Fall

With more experience, you can profit from falls by selling shares you don't own yet in anticipation of a falling price, in order to buy it back later on (hopefully at a lower price). This is called **short selling**. Term Short Selling allows you to buy it back any time over 11 months, while Day Short Selling is for traders to sell and buy in one day.

You can also minimise the potential loss on a declining share price by setting a price you would be prepared to sell at if it reaches that level (stop loss order). Investors nominate at what price they want their shares to be sold if the price goes below a certain trigger point. It is bounded by a limit price. Sometimes though, dramatic one-day falls can mean your trigger point is skipped. Then what do you do? Since markets tend to recover partly in the next few days after a market 'correction' (fall), reassess your choices then.

Louise Bedford, Director of <www.tradingsecrets.com.au>, says every investor should use stop losses, whether they do it manually or by computer (with a share trading program). Her view is: "If you don't know when you are going to get out of the market, don't get into it."

As an active investor you can set your own price level and then sell when it has dropped, say, 15% below the buy price. Do not make the mistake of holding on awhile just to see if it will recover, especially if the company forecasts are negative. A classic example: AMP in 2003. When it sank from highs of $24 down to $8, as an investor you might have thought at first, "they are a large company, I'll just hold on as it might turn around". The price then dropped further to $4, and you would still be waiting for it to return to high levels.

You can also lock in profits when you are not looking at the market. Using the same tool as stop losses, you set your profit margins through trigger prices and limit prices. CommSec call this Conditional Trading. For more information, see <www.CommSec.com.au: Trading Tools>.

Long-term investors with large portfolios tend to also use Options for protection. Options are derivatives that need indepth understanding, so I am not able to cover them in this book. Also see '*Using Derivatives*'.

> *Behind every man who gets richer quickly, there is leverage, and behind every man who gets poor quickly, there is leverage"*
> *– Marcus Padley (on ABC News, referring to Eddie Groves of ABC Learning and his troubles with margin calls on his stock's borrowings)*

Suggested Books:

For serious Australian share investors, check out:

Active Investing (2009), by Alan Hull.
Charting Secrets (2007, 2013), by Louise Bedford.
Let the Trade Wins Flow (2nd Ed, 2013) by Louise Bedford, Chris Tate, and Harry Stanton. Kindle ebook about a share trading mindset.

For would-be international investors, find:
International Investing: an Australian investor's guide to understanding overseas markets (2000), by Charles Beelaerts and Kevin Forde

Learning Points:

* To round up, taking your emotions out of share investing is very difficult, so you may need the aid of tools like stop

losses and dollar price averaging, combined with a common sense long-term view.

* To beat average market returns, you have to cull the losers and let the winners run. Many people have a tendency to do the reverse.

Managed Investments

Retail Managed Funds

Managed funds, previously called Unit Trusts, come in all types and break-ups of asset classes, under one or multiple managers. When you invest, you are really buying a number of units in the fund at their current market price, pooling your investment with many others.

If you have around $1,000 to invest, and ongoing contributions, there are plenty of funds to suit your needs. With $10,000+ capital, you can choose from most of the 5,000 funds on the market, although some funds have an even higher minimum.

There are funds for all levels of investor risk. It is important to invest in one that is not too high a risk for your comfort (such as geared funds), and to choose a suitable fund for the duration you need.

Investors pay their Fund Managers through an annual fee, called a Management Expense Ratio (MER). It includes fund management fees, trustee and custodian fees. The use of MERs allows you to assess the cost of holding different managed funds. Some managers also charge Performance Fees when their fund outperforms a certain index. Between 1% and 2% MER is normal, anything above that begs the question "is their performance worth it"?

One hidden cost is the '*buy-sell spread*'. This is the difference between a fund's entry price and exit price, and it is incurred each time an investor buys or sells funds. This is to cover the manager's costs (e.g. brokerage) that they incur on your behalf when trading the underlying asset. It is not very much, often about one cent difference per unit.

Check the fund for an ability to contribute monthly. This will come in handy if you decide to try instalment gearing, along with your own financial contributions.

The other thing to remember is your time to invest. Most growth funds recommend a period of holding of five years. This does not mean that you have to only invest for that time; only that it is riskier to invest for shorter periods, as you do not have time to balance out any negative or stagnant returns.

Tip: Normally people invest in retail managed funds through a financial adviser, but if you use a discount broker (e.g. CommSec, e*trade, or InvestSmart), you will get most of the entry fee (normally about 4%) rebated in units. If you do go direct to the Fund Manager, for retail funds they will charge you the standard entry fees.

Index Funds

Index Funds are another good way to diversify with a portfolio of securities at a fraction of the fees. You won't be hearing about these from any adviser, as they don't pay commissions. They charge lower management fees – less than 1% of investment value – as there is less active management (buying and selling) within the fund. Since the index manager matches the sharemarket index by buying shares in the same proportion as the size of the companies within the index (e.g. the ASX200 – top 200 Australian companies by market capitalisation), their performance only ever matches that index. So if the market heads down, so too will your wealth. On the other hand, in a raging bull market, index funds keep rising too.

Choose from Australian shares, international shares, fixed income securities, listed property trusts, or a combination of asset classes. They are also very tax-effective. Vanguard Investments Australia (www.vanguard.com.au) is a major index manager, charging from 0.35 to 0.9% MER, with no entry or exit fees. Most have a $5,000 minimum investment. Look under "fund performance - retail index funds".

In short, index funds are a great way to invest for the future without having to know anything about shares, take large risks, or pay a great deal in fees. They are excellent for any long-term purpose.

Listed Investment Companies (LIC) and ETFs

Listed Investment Companies (LIC) are funds that you buy through the ASX in the same way you do with shares.

Exchanged Traded Funds and other structured products are traded through the stock exchange. Exchange-traded products give exposure to shares or other assets such as commodities. Most

ETFs offer diversity for a low management fee (MER) of around 0.15 to 0.7%.

When you buy and sell units on the ASX, you pay brokerage (from $15.00). Options include a regular savings plan. Learn more about ETFs at http://www.asx.com.au/products/etf-and-other-etp.htm.

All exchange-traded products are designed to trade near their underlying Net Asset Value, so they offer fair value compared to the market.

As an active investor, you need to be aware of the main research houses: ASSIRT, Morningstar, and van Eyk Research. They all publish ratings on the quality and performance of managed funds and fund managers. Morningstar publish results in each capital city newspaper's 'Money' section or the *Weekend Australian Financial Review.*

When would Diversified Share Investing into LICs, Index Funds or ETFs be right for you?

If your main income is a trifle uncertain, perhaps as a contractor, freelancer, or self-employed trade, then these types of funds are a liquid investment that can ride with your circumstances – unlike direct property, which is not. Minimum amounts vary, but they all have low upfront costs (just brokerage) and tax-effectiveness of the underlying shares.

Saving for a child's education that is 10-15 years away, a Listed Investment Company or ETF is a low-fee way to enter the market, and tax-effectively invest in a package of 20+ diversified companies. Ensure you use the fund's Dividend Reinvestment Plan for a long-term way to watch your investment compound nicely. Buy and sell on the ASX with the fund's code, for the usual brokerage cost. Look for management fees of 0.3 – 1.3%, a fair price to NAV, and a good yield.

Specialist funds can give exposure to infrastructure (like airports or bridges), specific overseas stockmarkets, or international bonds. While many people get carried away with investing in Asian emerging funds, investors need to remember that specialised funds should be a small proportion of their total investment portfolio, to mitigate risk.

What's in a (Fund) Name?

If the fund has a name like "capital stable" or "conservative", then at least half of your investment is in fixed interest and cash. It has a defensive weighting and returns are low, growth minimal. "Balanced" funds have a diverse spread of asset classes and overall returns will likely be steady, but mediocre. If the fund were branded "growth", "high growth", or "emerging markets", we would expect those funds to produce higher returns in return for higher risk. Emerging markets funds invest in developing countries.

Imputation funds allow you to earn income with some exposure to capital growth from the underlying shares. This type of fund pays tax-effective income, since imputation has already been paid on dividends, and this tax credit is then passed on to you, the unit holder.

International Funds

Investing overseas means you will buy with overseas currency/selling Aussie dollars and vice versa when you sell, so you have double the volatility to think about.

Hedged global funds means they 'hedge' (or insure) against the movement of our dollar. In unhedged funds, when the Aussie dollar is on the rise it becomes harder to get good returns on international investments.

Hedge Funds

These funds invest in similar underlying assets as other funds, but they invest using specialised techniques, such as short positions, **derivatives**, and other exotic ways to invest. Hedge funds do well when the sharemarket is sliding, and they do just OK when the sharemarket is booming.

Fixed Interest

These are usually term deposit and mortgage investments. They are generally governed by the cash rate – the lending rate set by the Reserve Bank – but also by the value of the Commonwealth Government 10 year Bond (yield currently 3.3%). The gap is no longer very wide between the official cash rate and the average interest rate for deposit account-holders offered by the major institutions.

According to Canstar, the six-month term deposit for $1,000 at UBank is 3.6%, while the cash rate is 2.5% and the top online saver accounts offer 3.2 - 4.0%.

Cons: Fixed interest investors must ensure inflation and personal income tax do not erode all profits. Pensioners tend to rely on fixed interest because they feel it is 'safer'. Mortgage companies who offer unsecured lending are not a safe haven. You cannot benefit much from compound interest because inflation is busy eroding the real value.

Pros: At least bank deposits are generally a safe place to hold cash, and you can keep pace with inflation for a high level of safety.

Listed Property Trusts (LPTs)

These are property funds that are directly listed on the stock exchange and which own commercial properties, e.g. Mirvac, Multiplex, Valad.

In 2006 we saw property trusts outstrip shares, with the S&P/ASX 300 Property Trust Index averaging 34%. Listed Property Trusts swing from one extreme to the other, with high highs before a boom and low lows after a slump in the property market.

Property Securities Funds

Property securities funds invest in a portfolio of LPTs. This option suits investors who do not want the responsibility of choosing individual listed property trusts.

You can invest in property securities funds from a minimum of $1,000, depending on the fund manager. You may be able to add to your investment at regular intervals (savings plan). Check that you are able to reinvest the distributions, typically paid quarterly, if you would like to.

To invest in a property securities fund you will need to obtain a prospectus and, after reading the prospectus, complete the attached application form. Property securities funds commonly set entry fees or exit fees as well as annual fees. You can get a rebate on these entry fees by applying through a discount broker. Some funds offer a very low up-front fee, or no fee at all, and then impose high exit fees if you leave the fund in the early years of your investment. But many have no exit fee at all, so shop around.

Pros: Sector is quite low risk, with only one in 20 years showing negative returns. Suits moderate to growth investors, as part of their portfolio (through super funds or directly). Easy to diversify risk within the LPTs, but not out of this sector.

Cons: Long term buy, as LPTs are cyclical. Not as tax effective as Superannuation. Typically you will have to wait 4 or 5 days to access your funds when it comes time to sell them.

What about Super?

One important consideration for planning your retirement is where you will set up your Super fund or retirement account. All of the major financial planning groups in Australia do not actively recommend industry funds. This is because industry funds do not pay commissions to financial planners. There are many conflicts of interests regarding clear superannuation advice in the financial planning industry. You want all of the superannuation funds to choose from, not just those paying commissions. So how can you compare funds without any bias?

Perhaps compare Super funds online with research company SuperRatings.com.au. Their fund analysis and fund ratings cover the major industry funds, corporate, public sector, and commercial funds. They are completely independent but they charge for each rating report (from $39.95). Or do your own comparative research online with the help of your country's regulator (e.g. ASIC MoneySmart).

Confusingly, in New Zealand, Superannuation is the name for the Government age pension, while the KiwiSaver scheme stipulates both the employer (at 3%) and employee (3, 4 or 8% of before-tax pay) will add to a permanent worker's retirement savings.

Personal Superannuation has had a big push and a raft of changes in Australia, because the increasing number and future numbers of age pensions were seen as unaffordable for Government to pay out. Past rule changes included the ability to take out a lump sum or income stream (super pension) tax-free for those over 60.

Won't the Government look after me?

Most retirees today do *not* have enough Super, with 80 percent relying on a government pension to supplement their income (Source: Deloitte, 2013). Those born between 1957 and 1965 will have to wait until they are 67 to claim an Age Pension, while those born after 1 January 1966 will effectively be unable to claim the age pension until age 70 (and then pass the income & assets test). This means that you could possibly have age-onset arthritis affecting your ability to work but not be able to claim any age pension yet... a scary thought! However, you can normally access your own Super at age 60 (or 55 if born before 1960).

Many countries now give tax incentives to encourage sacrificing more money into personal retirement funds. A Deloitte report suggests that in order to have a comfortable retirement, Aussies will need to put an extra 5.5 to 7.5 percent into our fund voluntarily "each and every year", on top of the compulsory Superannuation Guarantee. Because this is difficult to achieve on a wide scale, plans for a slow increase in compulsory Super from 9.25 to 12 percent are already drafted.

Make sure that you have checked the projections of your retirement nest egg with more than one website calculator, and include your partner's details if you have one.

It is better to think of your Super as a source of income rather than a lump sum. Why? For one, because it's tempting to pay off large debts with a lump sum saved for retirement years. You also have to pay tax at normal rates once it's withdrawn and invested.

A Transition to Retirement Plan

With a transition to retirement strategy (**TTR**) you can access your Super earlier while you're still working. People who have reached their "preservation age" can draw on their superannuation benefits without fully retiring, but only as an income stream or pension.

Preservation age is 55 for people born before 1 July 1960. For those born after 30 June 1964, this increases to 60. If you are aged 55 to 59, you pay income tax on your TTR income, less a 15% rebate (and possibly less tax again depending on how the income stream is structured). You must withdraw between 4% and 10% of your pension account balance each financial year, no more and no less.

(!) A transition to retirement income stream must be an account-based income stream and cannot be converted into a lump sum.

Not all super funds offer these TTRs, so if you want to do this, look at all the options. If you have a SMSF, ensure the trust deed allows this type of income stream. (Any kind of trust complicates what can be done).

If you're already 65 or over, then you won't need to worry about a transition to retirement pension, as you can access funds directly in an account-based pension. And if you still work officially, then you could get your income tax reduced by contributing to Super before tax, while still receiving an income stream.

Voluntary Super looks attractive for employees on high incomes who salary sacrifice, as it is only taxed once on contributions at 15 per cent, effectively giving you around 15 per cent more money than you would have had in your net pay (depending on your tax rate). But if you salary-sacrifice into Super, don't expect any co-contribution payment, as you already achieve a tax deduction.

Rev up Family Super with a SMSF

On any Super fund, look at the various returns over the past few years. Did they come close to matching the sharemarket? Some people think they can do better for themselves, with more control, and so consider a Self-Managed Super Fund… with the help of a compliance agent.

In Australia, 1 million+ people are now members of a SMSF. A Self-Managed Super Fund (with a Trust Deed) lets you pool your assets for the one set of fees. For couples or individuals with over $200,000 in Super, SMSFs were found generally to be cost-competitive with retail funds, and with over $250,000 they were found to be cheaper cost-wise (Source: ATO.gov.au).

This is where an SMSF administrator or recognised accountant (holding a limited Australian Financial Services Licence) could help with strategic advice and compliance. It's not that easy to make SMSF decisions, so finding someone who will provide investing and fund allocation advice on a regular basis is a good idea. Incidentally, the concessional contribution caps change quite regularly, so it's best to check with a financial adviser or the tax office what it currently is.

How Much to Set up a SMSF? Establishing a new SMSF fund may cost from $550 to $1,500. To audit the financial statements and prepare the SMSF tax returns annually, costs range from around $650 to $3,000+ – but it depends on size and complexity of the fund, number of transactions, property involved, etc. The ATO supervisory levy and actuarial fees also apply. An example of the 2014 levy for ongoing SMSF funds is $388; reducing to $259. Consider the cost of advice on top of these fees.

Low-cost Self-Managed Super Fund Management and Auditing:

http://www.diysuperonline.com.au/smsf-services
http://diysuperaudit.com.au (Audits only)
http://www.onlinesuperfund.com.au/ (offers free establishment)

www.SuperGuide.com.au has crunched the numbers, and for couples retiring at 65 with $1 million, they would expect an annual retirement income of between $59,895 and $81,600 (depending on returns). For singles, it's between $61,600 and $69,440 – unless you expect to live until 100, whereby it reduces to $47,325 and $55,625 respectively.

Why Industry Super Funds?

Industry funds have low administrative fees and don't pay commissions to financial planners. Check recent asset performance in their core portfolio and look for those with a TTR. Recommended for funds under $200,000.

All types of super funds now offer MySuper: a default super fund with low fees and simple features. MySuper is what your employer will put the funds into if you do not offer your own Superannuation fund details.

What are you paying those retail super fund management fees for?

Roy Morgan Research estimates of June 2011 found that 72% of retail super fund members do not have regular communication with their financial planner. *(Source: 'Industry Super Australia - Snapshot of the Financial Planning Industry', 2011).*

In addition, many people do not realise which institutions own common financial planning companies, and so do not contemplate how that may affect the advice received.

Independent Retirement Planning Advice?

Business Name	Thought Independent	Owned By
Financial Wisdom	55% of clients	Commonwealth Bank
Godfrey Pembroke	50% of clients	Owned by NAB group
MLC	34% of clients	Owned by NAB
Hillross	44% of clients	Owned by AMP group

Source: Roy Morgan Research report, Money Magazine, Oct 2014.

Women and Super

Women's Super balances are generally half that of men, leaving them vulnerable in divorce or old age. After a long marriage has ended, uneven Super funds can be split in a divorce. Women often take years off or work part-time to look after their children and so their retirement funds are often less, leaving them at a disadvantage.

Since women often have lower Super balances than men, they need to pay special attention to it. During the period when a mother is not working, it would be ideal if their spouse could deposit a little savings into her super fund. Taxpayers who contribute for a non-earning spouse are eligible for an 18% tax offset on contributions of up to $3,000. Bonuses like the maternity leave payment could potentially also help the mother's super fund. Be on the lookout for new Government Super incentives for non-working mothers.

Other measures suit women working part-time. Whether single or partnered, while income is $34,488 p.a. or less, if you contribute $1,000 to a complying retirement fund after tax, the Government co-contributes up to a maximum of $500. For earnings over that amount, up to $49,488 p.a., the co-contribution reduces on a sliding scale. It is automatically paid.

Super for the Self-Employed

Did you know... the self-employed have around half the superannuation of employees. "Only 30 per cent of the self-employed aged 60 to 64 have more than $100,000 in superannuation, compared with almost 60 per cent of employees." (ASFA Research 2018).

While the self-employed are not legally required to contribute to a Super fund, it makes sense to set aside retirement savings. To combat the trap of 'forgetting' to add to Super, I ensure I put in $110 of net earnings automatically, every month, to my Super account through the Internet banking option.

If you are a sole trader or a partner, you will likely be able to claim a full tax deduction for your super contributions if business and/or employment income forms at least 10% of your total income. If you lodge a notice of intent to claim a tax deduction with your Super fund, do not also expect a Government Super co-contribution – you can't receive both.

If you make after-tax contributions of $1,000 to your super fund, with a total assessable income plus reportable fringe benefits, excluding deductions, of less than $41,112 in the 2021/22 financial year, you'll receive the maximum co-contribution of $500. So if lower-income self-employed pop in that $100 a month, it will soon add up and get a nice government contribution too.

Get a Flat 15% Tax on Super Contributions

Concessional contributions mean putting in employer guaranteed or salary-sacrificed super at a tax rate of 15%. The concessional contributions cap for the 2021-22 financial year is set at $27,500 for all ages.

For those with complying SMSF funds, they also have this cap (meaning only 15% tax is taken out on entering the fund). For them, unused concessional caps also roll over annually, for up to five years. (See ATO.gov.au/Super/self-managed-super-funds).

From 1 July 2021, for SMSFs, the non-concessional contributions cap will increase from $100,000 to $110,000. Members under 65 years old may be able to make non-concessional contributions of up to three times the annual non-concessional contributions cap in a single year.

Pros for Voluntary Super:

Complying superannuation funds receive tax concessions. Investment earnings are taxed at a maximum of 15 percent and capital gains are taxed at 10 percent, and then only when selling takes place. (Not applicable to tax-free super accounts).

Super payouts of any kind for the over-60s are tax-free in Australia. Super benefits from taxed funds withdrawn from age

60 will not be included in your assessable income. This means any money you receive outside of super is treated as though it is the only income you get.

Salary sacrificing into Super for high earners means they are only paying a maximum 15 percent tax. And because it comes out of gross salary, it may pull their total taxable income under a lower threshold.

Superannuation is a great way to save for your later years, as you are not tempted to dip into it. It's easier to take a long-term view.

Cons Against Voluntary Super:

You can't get it out until you're 60 or 65, or 55 with an account-based pension, unless proving financial hardship. If you're now under 45, that's a long time until you can benefit from it, and there may be changes of government rulings to Super, pushing it further out.

"The set and forget" policy many people have about their Super means that their money may not be in the best earning fund, so remember to check the asset allocation of your super fund regularly. Too many low earning areas (cash/fixed interest) will eat into your growth. Similarly, too much exposure to overseas equities increases risk (more years show negative returns).

You cannot use gearing in a regular super fund, meaning you cannot borrow to increase the growth of your Super. However, you can use gearing by instalments in a do-it-yourself SMSF. (Instalments are financial products that allow you direct exposure to shares by making a part payment upfront and delaying an optional final payment until a later date).

Inside an SMSF, you may gear to invest in real property, if for the sole purpose of providing benefits to the SMSF members when they retire (a lower loan-to-valuation ratio applies than normal, denoting a more cautious borrowing approach).

Tip: You should use the same principles with your Super as with any fund that you may own. Research funds, ensure spread of assets, invest small amounts spaced over time, ensure strong growth, and never sell out in a panic.

Learning Points

* Always check the asset allocation of your own Super fund/ Retirement Savings account. 'Balanced' may not be what you need.

* Industry super funds have the lowest fees and most offer personal accounts not requiring specific association within the industry.

* Women have about half (on average) in Super/Retirement funds than men do, so they need to plan and save carefully while in partnership and also in the event of divorce.

* People who contributed to their own Superannuation early in their working lives and who keep saving will benefit most in retirement, while those now in their 40s not ploughing in 15

to 19% in total a year (without an alternative plan) are apparently not even on track for a 'comfortable' retirement income.

* You cannot use the power of leverage within most Super funds; only SMSFs allow for gearing into shares or property (at a rate of around 60% Loan to Value Ratio).

Direct Property Investment

Why all the interest in residential property investing? Well, residential real estate has in Australia proven to increase its growth in value over the past 100 years (averaging 8% per annum, more than twice inflation). Now that's long term! It is also considered a relatively safe investment by the banks.

Since *Russell Investments* found that average investors in property only make a 4.3% p.a. return over ten years, even when gearing at 50 percent, it's obvious that investors are not making as much as they could.

Over the 10 years to Dec. 2017, residential investment property returns were the best asset, at 8.0% return (before-tax). Next best were Global Shares and Global Fixed Income, 7.2 and 7.1%.[7] Russell Investments warn not to try to pick next year's asset class winners, especially if you are going on last year's winner, because the winning sector always chops and changes.

7 ASX/Russell Long-Term Investing Report, July 2018

Why Negative Gearing?

Negative gearing is when the costs of holding the property exceed the rental return, thereby enabling a tax deduction for the difference.

So many people get overexcited about paying less tax. But when assessing whether to go ahead with a negatively geared property, remember, you must make a large enough capital gain (before tax) on your investment to cover all the losses you have made along the way.

The direction of property investment is changing in Australia, as people start to question negative gearing. At boom times, some advisers become concerned that many investors' negative gearing through property is too high. The risks are multiple: interest rate hikes, debt creep, a market slowdown leading to lesser capital gains… but most of all, it is the affordability factor that is of concern. Those with mid-range incomes can barely afford a rising cost to their bottom lines.

A less risky strategy for middle-income earners is to slowly increase property holdings when they have ample equity, finding properties that pay for themselves (are neutral) and offer good growth prospects. Also factor in interest rate rises.

Usually, a 20% equity holding in your principal residence is mandatory for a loan, and more than this, say 30%, will provide a buffer against bad times (e.g. rental vacancies, higher interest). You can also choose to only buy properties when you have enough for a 20% deposit in cash, to keep it really on the safe side, although this ties up some valuable funds.

Only 7.9% of Australians own an investment property. Most owners stop at one property, just 18% own two and 5.5% own three. Very few (2%) are property portfolio owners.[11] To me, it seems too risky to invest in one property long term (and pick it because you prefer that area). With no 'good little earners' to offset against any negative events or a poor buy, many battlers are leaving themselves open to debt servicing problems.

The risks of negative gearing are many: interest rate hikes, debt creep, a market slowdown, and lack of portfolio diversity

When mapping out your cash strategy, use a cash flow calculator or software to take into account your tax situation before you purchase. *DestinyLive* by Margaret Lomas has free tools to judge cash flow and yield, including depreciation deductions. (See DestinyLive.com.au).

Buying and Holding

Property prices cycle up and down like any other asset class, so you must be realistic and prepared to hold in stagnant or negative times. Buying in different States can spread your risk as often one capital is climbing while others are not.

If a positive or neutral cash flow property cannot be expected in your preferred suburbs, remember, in a high demand area the rising rents and rising equity should aid cash flow in the medium to long term.

[11] Onproperty.com.au – figures from ABS and RP Data

Bill Zheng of Investors Direct realised that many investors find it difficult in the first five years, so his strategy involves creating a positive cash flow even from a high growth property. On seeing their ad, I wondered "how can someone hold a high-growth property with positive cash flow while retaining the tax benefits of negative gearing?" Well, in the first five years the lender allows the interest rate to be reduced (say 3.5%, increasing 1% each year), thus delaying larger interest payments to when the capital growth has theoretically been achieved. However, the compounding interest means the debt rises, and if the property does not have good growth then the loan could have negative equity. It is a gamble that the market will keep rising by at least 4% every year and that the holding costs are not too much.

The mortgage interest rate is often talked about, as climbing interest rates put pressure on investors and retard some new buyers. While these factors can affect property sales, it is not going to stop people wanting to rent. Housing affordability, rental demand, and the housing price growth trend are key areas affecting Australian investors.

While Aussies love adding value through renovations, short-term investors (who do 'flips') are sometimes faced with a loss after selling, rather than the gain they thought they were going to receive. For wealth building, you must consider all the costs involved, not just the purchase and renovation costs. Your projections must include capital gains tax, land tax, stamp duty, deposit bonds, sales agent commissions, loan application fees and legal fees.

Tip: Do a capital gain projection using 10-year growth prediction figures from a market data provider… and look carefully at what type of housing is hot in your chosen suburb *before* you buy.

Again, patient investors usually win, as property markets often have surprise growth after a long flat spell, and no Capital Gains Tax is paid if you don't sell.

When, Where and What to Buy?

A strategy often recommended by leading property experts is to time your buying for the climbing period directly after a flat spell. Looking at the pattern of capital growth in various popular suburbs on the property valuation websites, you will begin to get a feel for it. It is free to check single suburb profiles on RP Data (www.rpdata.com.au), including median house prices, demographics, 5-year capital growth, unit prices, etc.

Residex (www.residex.com.au) and Property Value (www.propertyvalue.com.au) also provide useful paid reports on values, rental yields, and capital growth predictions.

Nearly half of all landlords invest in their own region "to keep an eye on it". And more than half of these aim to manage that property. Do you really need the headache just to save some costs? How about trying to diversify away from your own residential area? You can still visit twice per year, wherever it may be. You can also buy Landlords Insurance to help mitigate some of the tenancy risks.

Houses or Units?

Opinion is largely divided on this topic. Some argue that you can afford more units than houses, especially in capital cities. Units are easier to maintain. However, units often have higher vacancy rates, and also offer less capital growth (unless in high demand inner city locations). The costs can creep up on you, with strata fees and maintenance levies, so do your homework on the body corporate, starting with a look at the minutes of their meetings.

Houses are more expensive, but you can more easily add value through renovation without overcapitalising.

A townhouse might be a suitable compromise for those with a low buying limit, as they are an affordable buy in locations closer to a city. Never compare the price to a house on section in the same area, as the land value is not there.

Remember, land appreciates, buildings depreciate

If you want cash flow, niche market properties such as student accommodation, retirement units, or furnished holiday apartments provide high yields. But most lenders will be hesitant to lend unless the property has an alternative function – i.e. it can also be let to the general market if the niche market dries up.

So, look closely at the square metres offered in studio units, and also at what type of accommodation is generally sought after in the area.

Wealth Warning: Rural land buyers sometimes get caught with costs but no gain over ten years. If buying land, you must have a plan, know about council zoning in the area, and have a source of finance.

What about Commercial Property or Property Development?

These fields are higher risk in return for higher yields or profits. Michael Yardney (*How to Grow a Multi-Million Dollar Property Portfolio in Your Spare Time*) believes novices should take care in these areas. When asked why, he said,

> *"Simple renovations are a great way for beginning investors to start [since they add capital value]. Property development carries greater risks but potentially greater rewards. This strategy is certainly not for beginners and should only be attempted with the help of an experienced team. Commercial property has a different set of rules to residential investment property and is best left to more experienced investors."*

Some savvy investors have gained a steady cash flow by investing in commercial or retail premises, since the yields are normally higher, so if that is your goal you could always do more research and mentoring. There are a few more tips about this in my book *Creative Ways with Money*.

Sign up to Michael Yardney's free *Property Update* newsletter at www.propertyupdate.com.au.

Investing Your Equity Vs. Spending It

Have you realised the power of equity you may have quietly lying in your house? With an investor mindset, you could use it to leverage your way to financial freedom.

Say you and Ned (the spender) both have homes worth $350,000. You both owe $200,000, and you both apply to extend the loan back to 80% of valuation, or $280,000. Ned spends his $70,000 on an overseas trip, kitchen renovations, some new furniture and Plasma TV. You do your research and choose to buy a small property for $250,000, with the $70,000 for 20% deposit and costs, and mortgage of $200,000. It is cash flow neutral, meaning that no costs come out of your pocket. (Income tax deductions help with the ongoing costs.)

After three years, the value of Ned's $70,000 is a bit less than it was earlier (the renovations added some value, while the other things depreciated greatly). Except, adding the interest he paid on this borrowing makes the real cost $87,220 (8.2% pa). Now Ned has to work harder to pay this back. There is a lost opportunity cost as well, as this could have had good growth.

Meanwhile, your property is humming along at 6% pa growth, bringing it to a value after 3 years of $297,700. You now have the option of adding more value through renovating, or revaluing as is, and investing again.

Tip: There are many traps for unwary real estate buyers, whether it is their own home or an investment, such as not seeing auction 'gazumping' and failing to research the area. Find out more in

Neil Jenman's freebie, '*The 13 Worst Mistakes Made by Home Buyers'* at http://www.jenman.com.au or read his *'Real Estate Mistakes'* book in your library.

Learning Points:

* When considering property investing, look at it over a twenty-year period. While flipping may be temporarily exciting, it's also satisfying to accumulate lots of rental cash flow.

* Be careful of hidden fees when purchasing units in a strata, and also when buying through a property mentor.

* Negative gearing is not hot. Consider the implications if your income changes; diversify your portfolio and look to get your cash flow as close to neutral or positive as possible.

* Some people consider spending their home equity, but isn't it better to use it to invest wisely instead?

Protecting Your Wealth

HEADLINES: "**Investors fall prey to $1.5 million scam**. A Syndicate of Queensland investors has been defrauded of more than $1.5 million in a variation of the Nigerian money transfer scam."

Don't let yourself in for a fall. When someone offers you a wealth scheme or seminar, check out ASIC's consumer website: http://www.moneysmart.gov.au. This action could save thousands of your dollars.

Heavily-promoted seminars on Forex or CFD trading and high interest returns for mortgage lending schemes are just two to be wary of. The risk is very high, meaning your capital is under threat.

Always check that any financial promoter holds an Australian Financial Services licence. Do not deal with overseas brokers, 'solicitors', or other unknowns.

Spruikers with complaints against them include: Jamie McIntyre - 21st Century Eminis, Henry Kaye, Kovalan Bangaru, Brien Cornwell, property developer Keith James McCoy, jailed agent John Michael Talia, Kevin Young (ex-The Investors Club), Loral Langemeier (millionaire maker).

With new technology, there are even more ways to get scammed without leaving the comfort of home. Six-figure Internet affiliate programs, vanity poetry competitions, self-publisher vanity presses who inflate print prices while 'sharing' royalties (Arbor Books, AuthorHouse, iUniverse, Llumina Press, WinePress Publishing and Xlibris), binary options trading, Facebook-originated romance scams, cryptocurrency lookalikes, the dyed black money scam, money transfer requests, work from home scams, account requests (phishing) scams… all offer a variety of traps to fall into.

What do you do if you've already been burned?

Most people just opt out of investing completely and go back to working their job. Don't let the scammers and high-profiteers get you down.

Step One: Add an extra income stream, whether it's a micro business, or overtime, or consulting, and then gradually save again.

Step Two: Look at your budget, switch to buying good second-hand consumer goods, and cut back on some non-essentials (taxi travel, DVDs, lunches out). Check out trade disposal centres, op-shops and auction websites.

Step Three: Learn more about investing through books, and as your risk tolerance is likely to be quite low, stick to tried and tested styles of investing such as diversified property or lower-risk diversified funds inside of Super.

There are also now apps where you can go into property in very small amounts, called 'micro' or fractional investing, shared with hundreds of other investors. See BrickX or Spaceship. ETFs are also like this, but a little more established.

Structuring to Protect Wealth

Having full knowledge of investment structures such as trusts will help to protect increasing wealth. It may also help protect your estate from taxes and Will contesting upon death. Some people go to lots of trouble setting up a company to invest with, when the right type of trust is all they need. Others don't need a trust at all as they only have a small, non-risk-carrying service business, or they already have a SMSF.

Once you know which kind of trust you need, you can actually form and buy your own online. This is good if you need to take your time with the decisions and don't want a lawyer charging $500 an hour. The service at LawCentral (www.lawcentral.com.au) is a cheaper alternative, or LawDepot.com for US people. You will need to know the trustee names, appointers, back-up appointers, beneficiaries, and the settler, and know what assets you are going to set up or buy with the trust.

Of course, if you want to go to property trust gurus, you may end up with unnecessary complexity and high trust fees. But more likely you will use a trusted accountant. A top accountant will not only set up a trust well, with tailored advice, but will also help you maximise the benefits of the trust at tax time. Some even provide investor education. They should not set you up with a trust if you simply run a simple business with no plans to invest outside a few shares, unless there is a high risk of litigation.

The same is happening with SMSFs (Self-managed super funds) and the exorbitant fees of some administrators. Recent ATO figures show there are more than 1 million Self-Managed Super Fund members. Estimated expenses are in the range of 0.85 to 1 percent per year.

While you must be careful, DIY Super funds can actually save money in fees compared to retail funds if you have two to four family members' retirement money in it. You need someone qualified to administer it but be sure that the yearly accounting fees are not going to number in the thousands. Also get external advice before you go into any lending situation with the SMSF.

Pros of a Trust:

Protects assets from creditors and others taking legal action.

Unit or Hybrid trusts give control over who gets the income or capital returns. This can reduce the tax payable if split between different parties, as lower earners can receive the capital gain, and higher earners receive the income/losses. Beneficiaries can be added as necessary.

Family members' assets can be better protected from some de-facto or married spouses, who go to make a big asset claim when leaving.

Cons of a Trust:

Income must go to beneficiaries each year. Beneficiaries must pay tax at their marginal rate on all trust income distributed to them.

Some types of trusts (such as discretionary trusts) are best avoided for property investor taxpayers because of their inability to offset losses normally of benefit in negative gearing. (If the property makes a cash flow gain, then this is null and void).

If you already own assets and want them protected, it is costly to transfer them to a trust because of stamp duties and capital gains tax implications. That is why it is important to set up the ideal structure *before* you invest.

The Asset Protection Guide in print or eBook form is available from Trident Press, an Australian publisher.

Remember, setting up the right type of trust before investing can save on tax, improve flexibility in income diversion for business owners, and save your assets when it comes to litigation.

Other ways to protect your growing income and assets are:

* A valid Will (kept with legal person or somewhere safe). Save on fees by setting one up through The Public Trustee.

* Income insurance (tax-deductible or from pre-tax salary)

* Life insurance (cheaper through your Superannuation fund)

* Keeping a buffer of a draw-down or cash fund that only you can access when things have gone wrong

* Hold an investment in only your name if married (especially if you are a mother with young dependants), and

* Landlord's insurance for property investors.

Learning Points:

* Keep aware of scams and money rackets and the tricks that they use, like using testimonials, famous people, and greed. Get back on track with simple saving methods if you have been burned.

* Keep a valid and updated Will and insurance to protect your income and/or life.

* Gain further knowledge of the various Trusts before you invest in large investments.

* Consider the future for your family's wealth, such as gifting to children or gaining a new son-in-law.

Tax Deductions and Other Rorts

Under Australia's self-assessment tax system, you are responsible for declaring all your assessable income – such as dividends, distributions, rents, interest etc – and claiming only the deductions and rebates you are entitled to. Accountants can be of help, but please research any claims of tax benefits before investing, as you are solely responsible for the correctness of your tax return.

Look up www.ato.gov.au [Individuals]

Here you will find guidelines on what you can claim in your tax return regarding investments.

Offshore tax havens are at times promoted in Australia. The Tax Officer is fairly clear that any investment/transfer done to avoid tax will be clamped down on. Look up [Aggressive Tax Planning] [Tax Havens] [potential risk areas] if you suspect an evasion scheme.

Penalties for under-payment of tax are high, unless you come clean voluntarily.

Never invest solely for a tax deduction. The investment must stand alone as a solid area for potential growth. Also, if the ATO thinks that the main reason you are investing is tax avoidance, it may disallow the deduction and apply penalties.

"Do not negative gear investments for tax benefits; it's a mug's game. If you borrow to invest, make sure that you have to pay tax and that there is capital growth." – Peter Morley, Financial Planner

When considering splitting income to your children to lessen tax, remember that income in children's names has special treatment. They can receive up to $416 per year tax-free, but even distributions from a family trust that are between $416 and $1307 are taxed at 66%, and 45% over that. (Paper rounds—earned income—is considered excepted and thus taxed at adult rates). Teenagers who earn from jobs also might qualify for low-income or middle-income tax offsets if they don't also have major investments in their name.

Managed Investment Schemes

Hundreds of millions of dollars were invested in timber and agricultural ventures over the decade 2000 to 2010, thanks to the advent of managed investment schemes (MIS). Government initially enabled this growth by allowing investors an up-front 100 per cent tax deduction on their long-term investment. It took a few years to come back to bite investors, but bite it did.

Following the closure of 17 managed investment schemes in the forestry sector, other agribusinesses faltered, including mangoes, macadamias, olives, oranges, etc. The Government dumped the tax-effective nature of non-forestry schemes in 2007. There was a parliamentary inquiry into the agribusiness managed investment schemes in 2009, helping to put scheme members interests first in scheme collapses.

Just like subsequent managed fund recommendations, planners and other advisers were making fantastic commissions. Recent tax changes have helped to make the industry more transparent, with financial planner trailing fees stated and other legislation. Some smalltime investors have even received a cheque out of the blue for past no-service fees from their financial adviser.

Remember to always check with your accountant the current and *future* tax liabilities and benefits of any investment scheme you are considering.

Salary Sacrificing

Many employees are now sacrificing part of their salary into superannuation since it is taxed at 15% (rather than around 30 percent) and any earnings are also taxed at 15%. Please also read carefully about the pros and cons of Super (in Chapter 13).

Cons: Some companies won't allow you to salary sacrifice, and some are late in paying through the funds, costing you some interest. There are annual limits, and sometimes your compulsory super payments could be affected.

As Federal Budget changes announced annually (in May) affect the benefits of salary sacrificing, talk to your Accountant each year about this strategy. The book: "Funding your Retirement" by Max Newnham contains "growth in super fund balance over 1-40 years - salary sacrifice" charts, which make me wish it was part of my strategy as the outcome looks so beneficial.

Salary Packaging

At some companies they allow 'salary packaging' i.e. if your business use of a laptop, mobile phone, or car is included in your pre-tax salary. Motor vehicle packaging is not so beneficial, because it is regulated through the Fringe Benefits Tax system. If you work for a not-for-profit and they allow for some mortgage repayments or so on pre-tax, then it would pay to seriously consider taking up this option.

Your Accountant can advise you on which items are fringe benefits tax (FBT) exempt. Did you know that airport lounge benefits and 'living away from home' costs are FBT exempt?

Rental Properties and Taxation

Some people get caught in the trap of high negative gearing in a rising interest market. If any present property is causing too much cash flow shortfall, what can you do so that it becomes positive or neutral?

* Wait for the rising rental market to catch up with your costs. This could take some time, so only wait 3-5 years.
* Refinance to interest only repayments for a time, so that repayments are less.
* Do a cosmetic renovation (such as paint and new carpet), to add value and to attract tenants willing to pay a higher rent.

* Turn the property into a niche rental, e.g. furnished student accommodation or furnished holiday rental. These often have higher yields.

* Buy two lesser-priced properties and sell one high priced property. This is so you can sell one later on (when it has had some growth) to pay out debt on the other.

NB. Points based on Reno Kings' Paul Eslick and Geoff Doidge advice.

Even if your property is not costing you anything after tax, you can still claim most 'non-cash' taxation benefits, such as deductions on fixtures & fittings and building depreciation. Building depreciation deduction is given if built after September 1987 (2.5% of building cost for 40 years), or between 18 July 1985 and September 1987 (4% of building cost).

Extensions or alterations are treated as capital works and are depreciated in the same way. If not provided on the purchase documents, a quantity surveyor can work out a tax depreciation schedule for your property. In fact, they might find extra items you would not think of.

Learning Points

* Never invest solely for a tax deduction.

* People in the past investing in Managed Investment Schemes for reasons of tax deductions have been sorely bitten, so check for future likely complications.

* Get a quantity surveyor to work out a tax depreciation schedule for any investment property you own. The tax saved will likely more than pay for their charges.

* Consider salary sacrificing into Superannuation or a salary packaging option, if your employer makes this available. The self-employed can also contribute to their personal super and claim a tax deduction or else receive a co-contribution.

* Turn the tide on high cash outflow in a negatively-geared property by doing a cosmetic renovation and charging extra rent… or other creative strategies.

Advanced Wealth Strategies

If you are starting from a low savings base, there are many options for building wealth open to you. It depends on your objectives… is your goal to minimise tax, or is it to build growing capital and regular income in the future? The best investment will be able to meet all these objectives!

Option 1: Margin Lending for Shares and Managed Funds

Margin lending (or borrowing) for shares is feared by the masses, even by people who do not fear borrowing 90% of a property's value. This fear stems from the risk of margin calls: if the stock/fund value dips below your loan value, the lender asks for more funds or they sell units. You can reduce this risk by borrowing at 50% Loan to Value Ratio or below (borrowing at 33% is quite low risk).

If investing in growth stocks or funds, gearing is a building block of wealth that should be considered in light of your attitude to risk. (In income or balanced funds, gearing would not be advisable.) *Russell Investments* found that those who borrowed the equivalent of their principal for Australian shares made returns about 2% higher than non-geared investors, on average. (Source: *AFR SmartInvestor*).

When gearing into managed funds or shares, interest payments are tax- deductible. Those offering franked dividends give tax credits, which can then offset other income earned during that year.

Instalment gearing is a simple way to contribute monthly and borrow capital at the same time. Minimum is $250 per month. An example: if lender puts in $250 on top of your monthly $250, then it is 50% geared. You either start with $1,000 base or equivalent security. Select wisely and a growing capital reserve will be yours.

If gearing in a volatile market, try to hold a long-term view (i.e. don't look up your shares daily or weekly!) Remember though, gearing will increase your exposure to any losses in the market, especially if you sell on a drop or meet a margin call by selling part of your fund. This is the double-edged sword of leverage. Unfortunately, those investing through Storm Financial in 2007 were geared to the hilt, and many lost the equity in their homes.

Share investors who use margin lending need a real cash buffer in case of **margin calls**, or if desired, for ideal buying opportunities.

Read CommSec's brochure: "Regular Gearing Margin Loan" for more details about how instalment gearing works.

Option 2: Buying Multiple Investment Properties

For those who have already built up much equity in their own home, or a cash deposit, there is a good argument for buying solid property. Whether it's a house on scarce land near a city or furnished modern apartments (to increase cash flow), if you clarify your objectives, you will begin to narrow down your search.

You will need to buy more than one to fund a decent retirement income. The downside is, you must either manage the properties yourself or find an excellent property manager who will find the right tenants at the right rental price.

Good news for investors is that the national rental market is steadily growing, with vacancies in many Eastern cities falling below 1.5%, while home ownership declines.

Remember, not every property is going to have good capital growth, so if one of your properties is not looking like it will have good gains OR become positive cash flow within five years, then consider selling.

***Recommended reading*:**

How to Grow a Multi-million Dollar Property Portfolio in Your Spare Time by Michael Yardney, explains about how to choose properties for high growth. (Kindle $9.99).

Yardney's ***What Every Property Investor Needs to Know About Finance, Tax and the Law*** is a guide for Australians to the ins and outs of the system.

How to Achieve Property Success by Margaret Lomas, a compilation of three books, explains positive cash-flow investing. (Readers can download FinSoft, a property cash flow calculator designed for Windows, from www.Destiny.com.au).

Your Property Success with Renovation by Jane Slack-Smith (2012) gives a good overview of this strategy.

There are another two advanced ways to make money in real estate that you may not be aware of.

Option 3: Seller Financing (Wraps)

Many in Australia are unable to obtain finance for a home through traditional financing; but these battlers are hoping to own a home. The buying organisation will let them 'rent' a house for double the market rate and 'buy' this house long term at a high market price, regardless of market conditions. These and other Wrapping schemes have left many unwary buyers dissatisfied.

If you are in a good borrowing position yourself (i.e. a steady income and much equity in property), and are not afraid to negotiate with others, you could consider Seller Financing (Wraps) on a private basis. So how does it work?

As the seller or seller's agent, you advertise to those who want a home but cannot obtain regular finance. You earn a steady income from a small commission between what the banks charge and what your buyer pays. A locked-in capital gain is also set in the contract. Steve McKnight's property investing website has more details.

Option 4: Using Options to Buy Property

Using call options, you can make profits with little of your own money outlayed. Or you can use a call option if you don't have the correct legal structure or investor group established at the time of the deal, to give you more time before the contract of sale takes effect.

Basically, you can place an option (for a small amount) on any property, whether it is a house for $250,000 or a development site for $10 million. This is because an option contract gives you the *right* to purchase a property but not the *obligation.* For the bargain old house you might offer a $100 option, but for the development site you might offer say $500 per month for three months. You then have time to find a new buyer or group to exercise the call option by a certain date, or if the terms permit, let it lapse.

Options create massive leverage for you as the buyer, since you have some of the benefits of ownership without the pitfalls, such as mortgage payments, vacancies, etc. Close attention to the contract wording is imperative with Options.

> *"It's important for all buyers and sellers to fully understand and receive specific advice on these issues when using options. In particular, anyone using an option arrangement should be aware that the stamp duty treatment of options could be quite different state to state." – Mark Lyons, lawyer at McMahon Clarke*

The idea is you can on-sell a property without owning it, and make a profit. At a seminar, property option enthusiasts explain this system for utilising *call option deeds* in the marketplace, after some more tuition by them. This type of strategy relies on the 'optioner' to have skills in negotiation and links with possible buyers, unless they want to actually finance the entire sum on the option's call date. Hmm, can *you* build up contacts in the property development industry?

Using Other People's Money as a Deposit

No deposit? There are many types of "equity finance mortgages", whereby the lender offers an interest-free loan for up to 20% of the house deposit (most require you to chip in 10%). In return, the lender takes a portion of the future capital gain when selling, often 40%. It all depends on expected growth.

When your chosen area is in low growth (less than 4% annually), over a short time frame (say 5 years), this could put you in front, but in times of high growth, it would definitely not be a good idea. (Remember, over 100 years property grew at 9% on average). Also, if lenders cannot save anything while renting, paying off a high mortgage and costs might prove overwhelming. (Source: "Equity loan not equal for all" by John Collett, Sydney Morning Herald, 4 April 2007).

One alternative (for investors) is to save up the hard costs of buying a second property (often $17 - 20,000), and draw some equity in their home loan for a deposit, leaving a buffer. Lenders will only let you lend against 80% of home equity anyway. If you have that amount saved in the home offset account it also helps to show you're going to afford this investment.

Risky Lending Strategies

In late 2006, more than 5 per cent of loans issued in Australia were for above 95 per cent of property valuation, a high-risk strategy that had to stop. The credit crunch brought an end to many no-doc and low-doc loans, as well as an end to retirees' savings inside mortgage lending instruments (debentures).

> *"Research by an Australian home loan comparison site found 35% of mortgagees had felt the pressure of mortgage stress in the last year, with 10% attributing that pressure to a recent pay cut at work." (CreditWorld, May 2013)*

Using Derivatives, like CFDs

Contracts for Difference (CFDs), Warrants, Futures and Options (calls and puts) are all **derivatives**. These types of tools need in-depth knowledge and careful risk-reducing manoeuvres.

Derivatives are perhaps not the place to start, but feel free to gain more knowledge through the **ASX** or well-known investment authors. Don't be fooled by investment education spruikers who say "renting shares" – meaning options – is easy and low risk.

> *Where the upside is potentially higher, so too is the downside potentially lower.*

Managing a Complex Portfolio

It can get complicated to manage and track all different investments, including tracking performance of assets, tax benefits and liabilities, scrutinising yields and long-term returns. There are many software packages on the market that enable the private investor to handle these assessments.

Portfolio management software for large investors or regular traders is called Stator (http://www.stator-afm.com/).

For property investors, Jan Somers (author of '*Build Wealth through Investment Property*') sells PIA personal professional software, which analyses all the cash flow, capital gains, tax implications, after-tax cost and rate of return for any investment property (currently $245 for single user licence). See: http://www.somersoft.com.au.

Portfolios or Super funds can be tricky to manage. The Russell Investments/ASX (2018) Long-Term Investing Report notes:

"Investors often exhibit some common behavioural biases which have negative implications for their portfolios."

They found that over-confidence of humans leads them to trade too often; herding into a group means people tend to buy high/sell low; we prefer the familiar, so invest in our home country; we tend to separate money into accounts in a naïve sort of diversification.

They also advised to actively manage a portfolio full of diversified multiple assets, and find out the real return, i.e. the return after inflation.

Tip: In the Australian Stock Exchange's Education Centre, you can learn more about share investing, options, warrants, futures, bonds, ETFs, and experience trading in real market conditions with their Sharemarket Game.

See www.asx.com.au for a list of helpful educational resources. Alternatively, telephone ASX customer service on 131 279.

Returns on Investments

What kind of growth are you looking for?

As you become a savvier investor, your expectations for returns are likely to climb. After which, you might chase better returns. Every time the general populace forgets the last bust, roughly every ten years, there is a boom of some kind as people invest in whichever asset class seems to be making a good return. Tempered by the global credit crisis of 2008, this last property boom was hardly wealth-making stuff.

As well, Government policy changes can and do bring real returns down, either directly with new taxes on incomes, or indirectly, by affecting the investor market through business and consumer confidence.

Your own growth and income expectations should be in line with your investor profile and investment horizon (length of time you will hold the asset). Obviously you cannot expect huge gains if you are not also prepared to accept *any* loss of capital over the short term.

Those with decades of working life ahead can afford to take on more risk, as any negative returns will be evened out over time. As the active investor learns from mistakes made early on, he/she can streamline strategies and increase his/her wealth growth over the long term. But at any stage of life you can achieve your goals by starting small (even $500), staying within what you know or can learn about, and gradually increasing amounts with your growing confidence.

It has been said that you cannot get high yield, fixed investments without higher risk. Why risk your capital for a bit more? I realise many elderly people prefer fixed interest debentures/funds, arranged over the phone or with a financial planner. Retirees and families who lost their savings in collapsed mortgage funds, like Westpoint and ACR, expected their capital to be preserved while they earned a high rate of interest… sadly many large mortgage funds collapsed during and after the GFC.

In 2013, LM Investment Management went into administration, spelling losses in the millions for many pre-retirees. One of their funds, LM's First Mortgage Income Fund, was written down to 41 cents on the dollar then frozen. The result was a bevy of lawsuits aimed at both financial advisors' tainted advice as well as class action litigation against LM.

If investors had taken time to research the nature and inherent risks of that asset class, they perhaps would not have invested. If you have a fixed interest investment that is not with a bank, I urge you to find out more about it and its structure. Why? Banksia Securities, whom many Victorians assumed was a type of bank, was a financial services company who lent for mortgages, and investors lost in total $660 million when it collapsed. It was not covered by the Government guarantee on deposits nor the Code of Banking Practice.

As you gain more knowledge, you lower your risks

What is the Real Rate of Return?

When comparing returns of different investments, you need to consider the RRR. This means, what is the return after personal tax and inflation?

You might find term deposits or savings account interest not as good as you initially thought, because these offer no tax-minimising strategies and inflation is eating away at the real value. Over ten years to 2019, inflation rates averaged 2% p.a. for a total of 23%. (APH.gov.au) With tax, your real return could easily be less than zero from a term deposit bank account.

The type of asset has a significant affect on tax and real return. That's also why it's important to find out your net yield considering all taxation aspects involved.

Shares may have the benefits of both a good ongoing yield and tax benefits. If you are a low-income earner, then investing in shares with fully-franked dividends could put you ahead, as tax credits boost your overall income.

If your investment time horizon is long term (over 5 years), your portfolio can include capital growth assets like shares, real estate, and managed equity funds.

Tip: When you need an update on asset class returns, just download the *ASX/Russell Long-Term Investing Report* from www.asx.com.au and read their PDF (electronic file) for free.

Tax Benefits of Growth Investments

Tax-effective benefits from growth investments include imputation credits on shares, as well as depreciation allowances and interest deductions on property investments. The real rate of return makes direct property loans and margin lending into solid shares/funds with franked dividends (i.e. the company has paid 30% tax on them) look more attractive, despite the greater risks.

Over a 20-year period, the effective tax rate (after tax deductions) on Australian shares was about 21% for someone on the top marginal tax rate. The effective tax rate on residential property was 24%. In contrast, cash shows the lowest returns of all asset classes over 20 years, combined with its marginal tax rate of 34 to 38.5% for those earning up to $180,000 taxable income per year.

Capital Gains Tax (CGT). In the main, a capital gain arises if the capital proceeds from the CGT event exceed the cost base of the CGT asset. If the investment was held for at least 12 months in an Australian resident's name, capital gains tax is levied only on *50%* of the gain generated, resulting in an effective CGT rate of half of the individual's usual tax rate (only realised in the year you sell). Short-term trading incurs CGT at the full rate. Be careful when investing through trusts, as the CGT discount may not apply, as a trust is an entity. Complying Superannuation funds get a CGT discount of 33 1/3% for 12-months+ sales.

Voluntary superannuation is also very tax-effective, because it is only taxed once. It is important to monitor both the performance long-term and all fees of your super fund, to work out the real rate of return.

Return on Investment, and Cash-on-Cash Return

Pundits often refer to ROI (return on investment) – that is, the return an investment will give annually. You should estimate the ROI upfront before you invest. At the very least, you will want assurance that your initial capital will still be there. To judge the ROI, mark out two columns. On the positive side, put in all income, a growth estimate, and tax deductions, and on the negative side, list all the costs of buying and running the investment (such as fees), then adjust for inflation (3%), income tax if applicable, and probable capital gains tax on sale (dependant on how long you keep it).

If you keep it over 12 months, you'll get a 50 per cent reduction on CGT. You can decide whether to use the pre-tax or post-tax figure when comparing investments.

Some property investment authors use a similar reference called the Cash-on-Cash Return (CoCR), which enables you to gauge if your property is at least beating good bank account interest rates plus inflation. There are all kinds of costs, deductions and returns that you must include, and Steve McKnight's books have the formulaic table for working this out. Do not confuse this return figure with gross yield, which is often expressed as a percentage (i.e. 5%) by real estate agents eager to sell investment property.

Furthering your Investor Education

Now you have learned about the basics of wealth creation, it is up to you now to learn more about different areas of investing and start building up cash-flow… so that you can retire from the hard slog. To move towards financial freedom, I recommend reading any of these authors' books:

Alan Hull (active share trading)

Margaret Lomas (positive cash flow through property)

Michael Yardney (capital gain through property)

Noel Whittaker (sensible investing)

Rob Balanda (tax-effective trusts)

Nick E Renton (negative gearing, family trusts, retirement planning)

These authors are all down-to-earth investors/authors who are experts in their respective areas. Ideally, seek books written or updated in the last two years, as the way Australians invest has changed in accordance with superannuation and taxation reforms.

There are many Australian investment gurus offering different strategies. ***Steve McKnight*** and ***Margaret Lomas*** both endorse positive cash flow investing, representing good value in their books.

Are you still active? "***The Reno Kings***" in Melbourne have their unique way of adding value through renovating that you can learn in their book "*Real People, Real Stories, Unreal Profits*", articles or workshops. For a live, active style investor workshop, ***Cherie Barber**'s Renovating for Profit* course is ideal.

Michael Yardney's strategies in his books are very well researched over many years. He offers a range of low cost seminars through to advanced property seminars and mentoring.

Within share investing, there is ***Daryl Guppy*** (advanced trading with charts spawning strategies under his name), ***Alan Hull*** ("Active Investing"), and ***Louise Bedford*** ("www.TradingSecrets.com.au" and books, "Trading Secrets" and "Charting Secrets").

Where else can you gain an unbiased, well-rounded source of investor education?

Investors Voice is a researched quarterly publication of the *Australian Investors Association*, a non-profit organisation for investors. Investor members meet up around the country or chat online, and membership is only $110 per year. There are also occasional workshops, a managed investment report, and an annual conference.

There are many others teaching advanced styles of investing, e.g. *Jamie McIntyre (derivatives)* or *Rick Otton (property options/wraps): seminars banned in WA*. Their expensive courses and add-ons appeal to the get-rich-quick mentality, yet many learners have been left counting their losses. Before investing in education, take a step back and ensure you are not going beyond your own risk levels (or digging yourself into unrepayable debt).

While I have mentioned some options for novice investors to partake in advanced education or coaching, you really don't need to spend a small fortune to gain a well-rounded financial education; like I have, you can learn a lot by reading a variety of good investing books, websites, newsletters, and magazines.

A great way to learn: Investment Clubs

Another way many beginners enjoy learning about investing is in an **Investment Club**, where a group of friends learn together and usually advance to invest as a group in shares or managed funds. If you don't know of any clubs you can start your own. Here are the main organising steps:

1. Gather members and allocate tasks,

2. Choose and register your club name (check your State or Territory legislation as you may not need to),

3. Determine club structure and draw up partnership agreement

4. Determine operating procedures and rules,

5. Open bank account, register for a TFN, open account with stockbroker (if share trading),

6. Decide on how to split the operating costs,

7. File an annual tax return for the club.

Beware: *'The Property Club'* in Queensland is not a private investment club (Ex-TIC); it is a company selling high-priced new developments in a practice known as two-tiered marketing.

Recommended Websites

The Australian Stock Exchange offers newbie education, a trading game, newsletter, watchlist, and free online courses about ETFs, Warrants, Options and Shares:

www.asx.com.au/education/shares-education.htm

www.infochoice.com.au (home loan comparisons, online brokers, margin lending)

www.propertybooks.com.au (for books, courses, DVDs)

www.moneymanager.com.au (Fairfax Digital)

www.propertyinvesting.com (Steve McKnight's property forum)

www.propertywomen.com.au (women in property workshops)

www.residex.com.au (Residex Reports on residential property)

www.reiaustralia.com.au (Real Estate Institute of Australia: research reports, consumer info, and links to state branches)

www.superchoice.gov.au or superratings.com.au (Super fund choice advice) www.investsmart.com.au (free research for shares/funds/IPOs)

www.piaa.asn.au (Property Investors Association of Australia)

Investing Courses

Here are some options if you want to learn in-depth practical aspects of property investing from industry professionals:

Renovating for Profit (Sydney). Property investment from a buy, renovate and sell strategy with renovating queen Cherie Barber. Costs from $5,200, with a kit of templates and documents to get you started. www.renovatingforprofit.com.au

Property Planning Australia regularly offer a two-day Fundamental Property course suited to new investors in Melbourne and Sydney. TAFE SA (Adelaide) offers a comprehensive Property Investment general interest course, over 30 weeks.

General Finance:
For in-depth financial education, Kaplan Finance supplies a Graduate Certificate in Applied Finance (flexible delivery). Certain prerequisites apply. Apply at <www.seeklearning.com.au> search 'applied finance'.

Investment Newsletters

Happily for the DIY investor, most stock selection and investment newsletters offer free trials to entice subscription. Investors with active portfolios over $15,000 who are keen to have unbiased, expert guidance could make the subscription cost worthwhile. Some newsletters or guides are totally free.

MoneyManager Money Sense newsletter
www.moneymanager.com.au (all investing, free articles)

Intelligent Investor Share Advisor (share selection/education)
An online research service with a 14-year history of beating the market. Focus on the top 50 stocks and the next best 50 opportunities. Free trial. www.intelligentinvestor.com.au/

Michael Kohler's Eureka Report
Research articles, stock picks, EurekaTV, weekend briefing, and VIP event invites. Around $435 a year, with a free trial. www.eurekareport.com.au

Investing Times
Independent newsletter with long term view: sharemarket, fixed interest, property, retirement – good for SMSF owners ($250 p/a + GST).
www.investingtimes.com.au

Property Update by Michael Yardney (property & wealth, free)
www.PropertyUpdate.com.au

SuperSavvy, An unbiased, fearless Guide to Super
Mainly free. Compiled report is $19.95.
http://www.supersavvy.com.au

Investment Magazines

AFR Smart Investor (www.afrsmartinvestor.com.au) – Australian Financial Review's magazine for active Australian investors seeking information and analysis aimed at wealth creation and financial security. Also offer AFR.com – digital subscriber package.

Australian Property Investor (www.apimagazine.com.au) offers hotspots, case studies, property price data, legal issues, and property investment tips.

Your Investment Property (www.yourinvestmentpropertymag.com.au): offering hotspots, investment strategies and tips for residential property investors. See 'property advice' section online for good tips.

Tips to Remember When Investing

Be sure of *whom* you're investing with (the company/lender).

Be sure of *what* you're investing in (the asset type).

Know the *risk level* of the investment and feel comfortable with it.

Be sure you will make a *profit* within a set timeframe OR receive a good *income*, above tax and inflation.

Be sure *someone else is not profiting* more from your money than you are.

Be sure that *the risks are justifiable* for the promised rewards. (Or, if it sounds too good to be true, it probably is).

Take a *long-term approach* to investing when planning for retirement, and consider the *after-tax* and *after-costs return* for your situation.

I hope you now feel confident enough to regain control of your finances from your Financial Planner, Stockbroker, Accountant, or other professional. If they haven't been up to scratch, tell them "you're fired!" and start planning your financial future your own way.

Glossary

Asset class: Category of investment, e.g. shares, property, unsecured loans, hedge funds, bonds.

Asset allocation: Choosing the break-up of your investment portfolio. Also applies to superannuation funds.

Bear market: A market in which prices are declining for a long time and there is widespread pessimism (opposite of Bull market).

Bull market: A market where prices are generally rising. *Bullish* refers to the optimistic outlook that share prices are going to rise.

Blue chip stocks: Large, profitable companies with solid financials, e.g. CBA, NAB, BHP Billiton, Westfield, Coles, etc. Nothing short of global catastrophe would send them to the brink of failure.

Commodities: Resources including gold, silver, nickel, copper, petroleum, oil, or food products (wheat, corn, etc).

Compounding: A lovely miracle that happens over many years, when positive returns are reinvested. Compound interest is money that makes more money as the capital grows.

Correction: Euphemism for small value drop in index, often coming after bad news. (Crash being a large price drop in the market).

Debenture: A type of fixed interest security issued by companies in return for medium and long-term investment of funds, issued to the general public through a prospectus and secured by a trust deed. A debt obligation backed only by the borrower's integrity; an unsecured bond.

Derivative: A contract – the value of which is based on the performance of an underlying financial asset or index.

Dividend: Regular distribution of earnings to shareholders, paid in the form of cash, stock or script. **DPS** = Dividend Per Share.

Dividend yield: Annual percentage of return earned on a stock. Yield is determined by dividing the number of annual dividends per share by the current market price per share.

Earnings yield: EPS divided by the current share price. A way of giving the share investor's Return on Investment as a percentage.

Earnings Per Share (EPS): Calculated by dividing the number of shares into the profit. A growth company will have an increasing annual EPS.

Equity: Level of value that you actually own in your principal residence or other property. **Negative equity**: Home is now worth less than the amount originally borrowed from the lender.

Franked dividends: If an imputation credit (dividend) is fully franked it means that the company has paid the full company tax rate of 30% on the profits before distributing them as dividends. If the company doesn't pay the full tax rate, then its dividends will only be partially franked. Franking is a boon for investors, and low-income investors will be in for a good tax refund if they own lots of fully-franked shares.

Gearing ratio: The ratio of loan value to asset value. In real estate this is called “loan to valuation ratio”. A sensible LVR is 80%; that is 80% lending, 20% equity (or deposit). Margin lending for shares & funds is more likely to be 65% maximum gearing ratio, with 50% being a preferred level.

Internal rate of return: This is a return on investment that assumes all income received is immediately reinvested (allowing you to compound your cash returns).

IPO (Initial Public Offering): When a company first goes public management makes an IPO, making it possible for investors to buy the stock. Not every IPO is worth considering and has a solid future.

Margin calls: Where your portfolio’s lending value falls below the loan balance by more than 5%, a margin call is issued. As the loan-to-asset value is tipped down like a see-saw, your broker automatically sends a ‘margin call’ email or SMS to notify you to: a) deposit more money into your loan account to reduce loan balance, or b) buy more shares/fund units to increase portfolio value, or c) sell part of your portfolio to repay part of the loan.

Negative gearing: When the rental income from a mortgaged rental property is less than the interest on borrowings plus expenses, thus causing the investor to pay some money from his/her after tax income. Interest and other ordinary expenses of holding the property are allowable tax deductions against all income the investor earned in the year.

Positive cash flow: When rental or other income is greater than associated expenses, after personal income tax is taken into account.

Positive gearing is when raw income exceeds raw expenses.

Preferred stock: Ownership shares, issued initially by a company and then traded by investors.

P/E ratio (Price to Earnings ratio): This measure is worked out by dividing the current share price by the company's annual Earnings Per Share. The higher the P/E ratio is, the more positive the market views the future earning potential of the company.

ROI (Return on Investment): The ROI is a return ratio that compares the net benefits of a project versus its total costs (profit or loss). Expressed an annual percentage return.

SMSF (Self-Managed Superannuation Fund): A fund governed by yourself as trustee, still abiding by the rules of compliance and preservation.

Sector correction: A correction is a crash that brings overvalued companies (this time in one sector) back down to earth. Ripple effects usually cause a major market dip, such as the Tech crash of 2000.

Short selling: To short a stock, an investor buys shares under a contract, giving them ownership of the stock temporarily, then sells the shares with a view to buying them back at a lower price. They profit from the difference once the "borrowed" shares are returned, providing the price hasn't risen in the meantime. Also used to protect a profit in a 'long' (usual) position.

Stapled securities: Stapled securities are a form of equity securities comprising two or more different entities (e.g. a trust and a company) that can only be traded together as if they were a single security.

Speculative stock: A publicly listed company that has yet to be proven. Commonly in mining or biotechnology. May seem cheap, but is inherently risky as the market swings it in and out of favour. Also known as "penny stocks" due to the small price per share.

Volatility: The degree of fluctuation in share prices, exchange rates, etc. The greater the volatility, the less certain the investor's return.

Yield: Return on investment in percentage form. In property, as rents rise, so do yields. Higher yields generally mean more money in your pocket. Most figures quoted disregard personal taxes.

Appendix A - Family Financial Planner

1. Savings Balances & Goals

Current high interest savings balance:

Current transaction account balance:

Super balances:

Goal 1:

{e.g. Build up Emergency Fund, $250 p/m ongoing}

Goal 2:

{e.g. Save $150 pm for new car for 18 months}

Goal 3:

{e.g. Save $65 pm into Education fund, ongoing}

Goal 4:

{e.g. Save $100 pm for next holiday in December 2008}

2. Income

Estimated family income: gross: $ less tax: $

Rental, dividends, rebates income:

Business/employment income goals:

3. Super, Shares & Managed Investments

To add $................ this year to ....'s super.

To add $................ this year to ....'s super.

Based on our contribution, Govt. co-contribution:

....

Assess super in .... months. Due:

Assess shares/funds every (six?) months. Research whether to sell, buy or hold. Shares/Funds value (30 June …) $

Capital growth ....

- Any losses .... = Present value $ ....

4. Property Plans

Change monthly repayments to fortnightly OR add 10% additional repayments OR get offset/line of credit account.

Pay out mortgage by ....

Buy ___ investment properties in (month, year) ....

5. Protection

Take out life insurance on ………, payout $…00,000. Premium:

Reassess life insurance on ………, payout $…00,000. Premium: (Don't forget to add in costs of childcare, housekeeping and loss of income for a few years)

Optional Income Insurance: premium $…… per month, waiting period …. months. (Can be deducted by employer).

Set up a Will or assess current Will for additional assets and life changes.

Build up emergency fund of $……..... in a cash account (online saver).

Assess whether future investments would be better under a type of Trust.

(Like a MS Word copy of this to avoid much typing? Email: Jennifer@jenniferlancaster.com.au for a free Financial Planner file).

www.ingramcontent.com/pod-product-compliance
Lightning Source LLC
Chambersburg PA
CBHW060027210326
41520CB00009B/1031

* 9 7 8 0 9 9 4 5 1 0 5 7 0 *